Working With dBase II

Working With dBase II
The Personal Computer Database

M. de Pace

GRANADA
London Toronto Sydney New York

Granada Technical Books
Granada Publishing Ltd
8 Grafton Street, London W1X 3LA

First published in Great Britain by
Granada Publishing 1984
Reprinted 1984

Copyright © 1984 by M. de Pace

British Library Cataloguing in Publication Data
De Pace, M.
Working with dBase II.
1. dBase II (Computer program)
1. Title
001.64'42   QA76.9.D3

ISBN 0 246 12376 1

Typeset by V & M Graphics Ltd, Aylesbury, Bucks
Printed and bound in Great Britain by
Mackays of Chatham, Kent

All rights reserved. No part of this publication may be reproduced, stored in a retrieval system or transmitted in any form or by any means, electronic, mechanical, photocopying, recording or otherwise, without the prior permission of the publishers.

Contents

Preface		ix
Part 1: Simple dBase II		
1	Introduction	3
	What is dBase II?	3
	What does dBase II provide?	4
	dBase II and the personal computer	5
	Starting dBase II	6
2	Storing Your Data	9
	Choosing an application	9
	Designing the file	9
	Creating the file	11
	Entering data	12
	Editing data	16
3	Listing Your Data	19
	Listing records	19
	Creating a report	22
	Locating files	27
4	Working With Your Data	28
	Getting the data into sequence	28
	Working at the screen	33
	Counting and totalling	37
	Review	40

Part 2: Additional dBase II Techniques

5	Changing Your Mind		43
	Inserting records		43
	Deleting records		44
	More editing		47
	Changing the database		50
6	dBase II in Business		53
	A business application		53
	Updating one database from another		53
	Using two databases		57
	Copying and joining databases		59
	Review		62

Part 3: Programming with dBase II

7	Writing dBase II Programs		67
	What is a dBase II program?		67
	How to start		68
	Programming a report		70
	Writing an enquiry program		81
	Pictures		87
8	Programming Your Work		91
	Updating from the screen		91
	Format files		96
	Creating a menu		99
	Name and address labels		103
9	Going Further		110
	Macro substitution		110
	Memory variables		114
	Preparing invoices		117
	Validating the date		123

10	Functions and Techniques	128
	Functions	128
	SET commands	135
	Special techniques	138
	Documentation	143
11	Linking With Other Programs	146
	External files	146
	Command generators and utilities	148

Appendix A: dBase II Program Files	152
Appendix B: Word Processing and dBase II	153
Appendix C: Summary of dBase II Commands	155
Appendix D: dBase II Constraints	168
Index	169

Preface

dBase II is commonly accepted to be the market leader in databases for the personal computer. It owes this prominence to the fact that it is simple to use, yet extremely powerful and flexible. It is also a very effective organiser of anybody who has to store information and who is in some way dependent on the use of that information. People find that they can breathe a sigh of relief because they have been released from the tedium of keeping track of everything, or from having to sift through mountains of detail to find the answers to a few simple questions.

As a long-standing user of both IBM and other mainframe computers, and as a supplier of computer services to my company, I found the ease and sophistication of dBase II refreshing. I delighted in the quick implementation of solutions to user problems that it made possible. Since the package was so friendly, I decided to pass dBase II on to my computer users to try for themselves. The next step was to collect material on the package which would enable the users to get a thorough grounding in the facilities available to them.

That step was never taken. There were only two books published on dBase II, and neither met our requirements. Nor did the users feel happy with the Ashton-Tate documentation which accompanied dBase II. In the end we managed without. This book was born out of that experience. I hope it will be found to be inviting to the casual user, yet thorough.

The material has been presented with the first-time user in mind, but illustrations have been provided which will enable those familiar with dBase II to use the book as a ready reference guide. All dBase II keywords have been sign-posted with illustrations in the margin. dBase II commands are indicated by a screen, dBase II files by a floppy diskette, and dBase II functions by a square containing the 'f' function sign. Each illustration contains the appropriate dBase II keyword.

The Summary of dBase II Commands which is given as Appendix C has been reproduced by courtesy of Ashton-Tate, who produce dBase II. David Imberg, the Managing Director of Ashton-Tate (UK) Ltd, was particularly kind in looking through the manuscript and permitting us to use the dBase II logo on the front cover.

Trademark acknowledgements, other than those given in the text, are as follows: Wordstar is a registered trademark of Micropro International; Supercalc is a registered trademark of Sorcim Corporation; 1-2-3 is a registered trademark of Lotus Development Corporation; CP/M is a registered trademark of Digital Research Inc.

M. de Pace

Part 1
Simple dBase II

Chapter One
Introduction

What is dBase II?

Few people realise what impact a personal computer coupled with a powerful database package like dBase II can have on their lives. Databases are usually associated with storing and retrieving information, which indeed describes part of what they do. What is not generally understood is that dBase II plus a personal computer can organise you in much the same way that an extremely efficient secretary would. Suddenly your letters are automatically produced for you, your invoicing is up to date, your record keeping is under control, and when you need to know something fast, it is readily available. There is tremendous satisfaction in being able to walk up to a computer, tap in your requirement, and with no delay have the necessary details given on the screen or printed on the printer. Nor is there the frustration of listening to very good reasons why you cannot have the information you need. The user of dBase II finds that less time is wasted on long and unprofitable exercises and more time is available to spend on the really essential aspects of the business.

The domestic user of dBase II will find that similar benefits are available. If you have information that you want to put under control, particularly the kind that you might wish to look up quickly, you will find an organiser like dBase II very useful. Being general-purpose and easy to put to work, you will find that dBase II lends itself to solving most of your information problems.

Why is it called a database?
A database is a *file*. A file is a collection of data stored on a magnetic

medium such as a diskette, and identified by a filename. How, then, are databases distinguished from other files?

The answer could be lengthy but what it boils down to is that a database is a file that comes accompanied by supporting software which does most of the dirty work for us. For example, the database program maintains a dictionary for each database file which tells it where on a record each fieldname is stored, how long it is, and what kind of information – whether numeric or character, for instance – the field contains. All we have to do is to use the fieldname in our processing without concerning ourselves about the boiler-room activities which take care of such mundane matters as locating the field on a record, moving it to a working store for processing, and generally doing all the low-level work.

Do not think, while you are unconcernedly issuing commands which do a hundred and more things with the data, all of which would have cost you dearly in BASIC or COBOL, that the low-level work has somehow disappeared. It is still very much there but has been so successfully integrated with the data dictionary and other features of the database program, that you no longer notice it.

To the first-time computer user, a database program offers a means of obtaining substantial benefit from his computer without having to tread the time-consuming and complex world of computer programming languages. With almost no preparation, he is suddenly in there with the rest of them, processing his records and producing stylish reports and wondering why he had not thought of making life so easy, years before.

What does dBase II provide?

You will see as you proceed through the material in this book that you are offered three levels of using dBase II, in Parts 1, 2 and 3.

The first level covers no more than twenty-five commands which tell dBase II what you want it to do. Yet it will enable you to create a database, enter information, change details afterwards, produce simple listings or formatted reports, and use the computer screen as a means of delving into your information in order to answer enquiries.

The second level is a minor progression from the first. It covers a further fifteen commands which add sophistication to what you have already learnt. These also enable you to manipulate databases, both in the context of changing your mind in respect of what you want them to contain and in processing more than one database at the same time.

When you have mastered the first two levels, in Parts 1 and 2, you may stop. You have been supplied with a comprehensive package of tools which you may apply with ease to the processing needs of your domestic or business environment and which, by any other means, would have required a considerable investment in time and money. The forty or so dBase II commands you will have already covered by then, might be as far as you need to go.

The third level, in Part 3, requires logical thinking at a detailed level, and begins to approach the standard computer programming languages, albeit not at the lower level of maintaining files. You are here introduced to the dBase II procedural language. Again, it does not involve more than 20 or so new commands. The language is simple. The concept of using commands in a procedural fashion may not be so simple, but when you have read to the end of the material in this volume you will find it no more difficult to use than the early, simpler commands. It will enable you to set up screen menus, produce pre-formatted printed documents such as invoices, format a screen for a non-technical user to enter information, write enquiry routines for non-technical users, and generally put information within the reach of its users without requiring them to become proficient in technical matters such as the use of a database.

dBase II and the personal computer

dBase II is available on a large number of personal computers. This does not mean, however, that the dBase II program which runs on a Superbrain can be transferred to an IBM PC. Computers are not designed to a common standard, so that the signal which activates, say, a screen operation would be different from one computer to another.

To allow a program such as dBase II to run on a variety of computers, different versions of the program are produced, each tailored to a specific computer. When purchasing dBase II, you need to specify which version you want, Superbrain, IBM PC, etc. You then receive the program on a diskette which can be read by your computer and the program will be compatible with the operating system of your computer.

There are several different operating systems. The best-known is CP/M which stands for Control Program for Microprocessors.

With few exceptions, CP/M has become the standard operating system for 8-bit personal computers such as the Superbrain. It consists of a number of programs which typically reside on a diskette to be called up as required when the user issues a command. The programs take care of finding files, loading programs, saving memory, copying files, etc.

Another well-known operating system is MS-DOS which was developed to run on 16-bit computers such as the IBM PC and the Victor 9000/Sirius. MS stands for Microsoft (the company that produced the system), and DOS stands for Disk Operating System. IBM called their version PC-DOS after the initials which identify the IBM personal computer.

The CP/M system has also been extended to work on 16-bit computers and that version is known as CP/M-86 after the INTEL 8086 microprocessor chip which with its variant, the 8088, forms the basis of many 16-bit personal computers. The 8-bit CP/M, in turn, has been retitled CP/M-80 after the INTEL 8080 and Zilog Z80 microprocessor chips which form the heart of most 8-bit personal computers.

dBase II itself has been through a number of versions as a consequence of improvements or tailoring for a specific operating system. Thus, version 2.3B is dated 22nd February 1982, version 2.3D is dated 29th November 1982, and version 2.4 is dated 1st July 1983. Database files created by one version will be compatible with the next, but a newer version may prevent earlier command files, i.e. dBase II commands stored on a disk, from running correctly. This is not a serious problem since the number of commands affected in this way are usually few and the documentation which arrives with a new version provides a clear and separate list of all changes. There is, of course, no reason to move on to a new version other than to obtain the latest facilities.

New versions are available as they appear, either free or for a small charge, to any purchaser of dBase II. When you purchase the package, you should complete and return the licence agreement to Ashton-Tate, the producers of dBase II. That will register you with them as a user and entitles you to receive new versions and news on developments concerning the package.

Starting dBase II

The program is loaded by entering DBASE against the CP/M or

Introduction 7

DOS prompt and pressing the return key. The program will load from the diskette and then display the following:

ENTER TODAYS DATE AS MM/DD/YY   OR RETURN FOR NONE :

You may ignore the date by pressing Return which will store a date of 00/00/00. The date is added to your files when you write to them to help you keep track of their use, so it is advisable to enter the correct date but you do not have to. The above applies to CP/M versions of dBase II, since the DOS version will take the date from the DOS date store instead of waiting for you to enter the date.

The program will next display the version number. For example,

   ***   dBASE II   Ver 2.3B   22 FEB 82

The date beside the version number shows you when it was issued. (The material in this book is based on versions 2.3B onwards.)

The version number is followed by the dBase II prompt. By now you are probably familiar with the prompt given to you by CP/M and DOS, which invites you to enter a command such as DIR to look at the files on a diskette. dBase II has a similar prompt, but it is so modest that one may be forgiven at times for not noticing it. It consists of a single full stop or dot at the left of the screen.

The dot is your invitation to talk to dBase II, using one or more of its eighty-plus keywords as a communication medium. As you will see shortly, you can go a long way by using no more than a dozen commands.

When you go wrong, dBase II will inform you, by means of its error messages, where you have not followed the rules. It will also in certain cases try to help you by allowing you to correct an attempted command. If, for example, you incorrectly spell the name of your file and the program cannot find it, the following will appear:

   . use bookd
   FILE DOES NOT EXIST
   use bookd
   CORRECT AND RETRY (Y/N)?

Having told you that the file does not exist, the program reproduces your command and then offers you the opportunity of correcting it. If you reply 'N', the dot prompt will reappear and you can start from scratch. If you reply 'Y', you will enter a dialogue as follows:

   CHANGE FROM   :bookd
   CHANGE TO   :books
   use books
   MORE CORRECTIONS (Y/N)? n

The error correction dialogue is particularly useful when a series of dBase II commands are executed from a diskette file, and one is able to correct on the spot rather than being forced to edit the command file before being able to try again. Very often an attempt at an error correction does not succeed the first time; dBase II will quite happily allow you to try and correct the error as many times as you wish.

For single commands, with the exception of a few situations where it is nice to be able to correct rather than re-enter the whole line, the error correction dialogue is not really necessary. It is, however, necessary to be aware that it will appear frequently and that one should be able to deal with it. You can always enter N if you do not want to use it.

Version 2.4 of dBase II contains a HELP command which may be used to check on the structure of a command without moving away from the screen. For example,

. help use

The HELP command will display the structure and options of the USE command and provide a brief description of the command.

dBase II commands come in many sizes. Some are short, such as USE, while others are long, such as DISPLAY STRUCTURE. Once you have become familiar with the commands, you will find it tedious to enter the longer commands in full. You may, therefore, prefer to use the abbreviated form which consists of the first four letters of each word, e.g. DISP STRU.

Certain commands allow you to specify a list of items. If the list is a long one, it could run over a line. When this happens, finish the first line with a semi-colon. That will tell dBase II that there is more to come on the next line. There is no fixed position for the semi-colon; it is simply placed after the last character on the line.

With this minor bit of preparation out of the way, you may proceed to use the program and will, without a doubt, find yourself impressed by its ability to provide solutions to your processing problems with a minimum of effort on your part.

Chapter Two
Storing Your Data

Choosing an application

The application which has been selected to illustrate the use of dBase II in its basic mode is a simple one: keeping a record of the books in a house.

We will assume for the purpose of this illustration that there are four bookcases in the house: one in the hall, one in the lounge, one in the dining-room, and one in the study. We want to keep a record of each book, showing not only the author and title, but also the classification (e.g. Travel, Biography, etc.), the location of the book, and for the sake of including an arithmetical detail in our illustration, the cost of each book.

The records would be used variously to list all the books in a certain classification, say, all the Cookery books; to find out which bookcase contains a specific book; to find out whether there is a book by a certain author; to compile a full list of all books; to find out how much we have spent on computer books; and so on. Later, this example will be converted to that of a bookseller running more than one shop, to provide us with an illustration of dBase II in a business environment.

If you are a business user and you find yourself tempted to skip past this early part because of its domestic setting, just adjust your viewpoint slightly. For 'books' read *stock*, for 'location' read *warehouse* or *shop*, etc., and you will find that these database techniques apply equally to the needs of the home, the factory, the shop, and the office.

Designing the file

The first task is to decide what information we want to store and the maximum size of each piece of information. Bearing in mind that we are keeping to a simple illustration, we decide on the following:

```
Title          :   40 characters
Author         :   25 characters
Classification :   15 characters
Location       :    6 characters
Cost           :    5 characters

Total size     :   92 characters
```

Each item of information is known as a *field*, and the collective name for the fields representing a single entry, i.e. one book in our example, is a *record*. You will see that the total size of the information for each book is one character larger than the sum of the individual field sizes. dBase II needs the extra character to store information about the record.

The next thing to do is to consider how many books we expect to load. If we have, say, 500 books, the size of our file would be approximately 92 times 500, or 46000 characters. (On top of that there are some 500 characters which are used to store the details of the database structure.) On an IBM PC diskette, which provides approximately 320000 characters, there would be ample space. If, however, there were 5000 books, the file would occupy 460000 characters and one would then consider using a hard disk giving 5 or 10 million characters of available space, or breaking the information up into two or more logical groups. You might, for example, decide to keep all the fiction on one file and all the non-fiction on another, using one diskette for each category. It is important to have spare space available on a diskette to allow for additions to the file. The number of potential additions will depend on the application: in our illustration, we would not expect to add more than, say, 5% each year. Another possible cause of the file expansion is the addition of an extra piece of information in respect of each book. If we decided afterwards to add the name of the publisher and used 9 characters per book to do so, we would be increasing the overall file size by nearly 10%.

The dBase II software files require approximately 60000 characters in version 2.3 and 70000 characters in version 2.4, leaving in rough terms 80% of an IBM diskette for files. In fact, version 2.4 uses an extra 52000 characters for its HELP file (DBASEMSG), but you need not have this file on your diskette if you are pushed for space. As you will discover later, there will be a need for indexes and

Storing Your Data 11

other work files in addition to the main data file. If the latter is likely to occupy most of the space on a single diskette, it is advisable to hold it on a separate diskette in the B: drive.

Creating the file

Once dBase II has been entered, it responds with a dot or fullstop and waits for you to enter a command. In this case, enter CREATE. You will then be asked for the name of the file. We have decided to call it BOOKS, so enter that. Remember that CP/M and DOS restrict filenames to 8 characters. If you want your file on the B:drive, prefix the name with B:. The CREATE command and the filename could be supplied at the same time:

. create books (or b:books)

Next you are asked to enter the record structure, i.e. the details to be stored. Enter the name, type, and size of each piece of information. Type defines the information as being 'numeric' or 'character', the latter being digits and letters mixed. Once you have entered these details, the file will be created and there is no more to do other than to type in the actual information itself – the titles, authors, etc., of the books.

The sequence of creating a file looks like this:

```
.create
ENTER FILENAME: books (or b:books)
ENTER RECORD STRUCTURE AS FOLLOWS:
FIELD        NAME,TYPE,WIDTH,DECIMAL PLACES
001          title,c,40
002          author,c,25
003          class,c,15
004          location,c,6
005          cost,n,5,2
006          <CR>
```

The fieldnames may be up to 10 characters long. You will see that on Field 5, the type was given as 'n' (i.e. numeric), and the width as 5 with 2 decimal places. Describing a field as numeric allows you to perform arithmetic on it such as totalling up the cost of all books in a given classification. The width of a numeric field is a bit more complicated than that of a character field. If you are using decimal places, the width includes the decimal places and you also have to allow an extra position for the decimal point itself, i.e. a width of 5,2 will allow a maximum value of 99.99. Moreover, if you anticipate using negative amounts, you have to allow an extra position for the minus sign. Thus −65.95 will occupy six character positions so you would enter the width as 6,2.

There is a third field type which is not illustrated here, but which you should know about. It is known as a 'logical' field, and may contain a single character only. You use logical fields as indicators, i.e. they contain Y or N for yes or no, or T or F for true or false.

Throughout the examples in this book, your entries will be shown in lower-case and the responses of dBase II in upper-case. In practice, however, you are free to use either lower- or upper-case. The field numbers are supplied automatically to prompt you to enter the next item: pressing the return key without entering any information, as on Field 6, signals to dBase II that you have completed your entries.

The filenames of all database files created by dBase II are suffixed by .DBF, so the program will now write these details at the front of a file which is called BOOKS.DBF, and then ask you if you want to start entering data to the database file, i.e. type in book details. Type N for the moment. The dot will reappear, waiting for your next command.

In order to show you how you leave dBase II, let us assume that you are satisfied with your efforts in creating a file and that you want to switch off for a while. You should never leave dBase II by switching off the computer. You always give the program a chance to tidy itself by entering the exit command, which is as follows:

. quit

When you enter information dBase II does not always immediately write this data to the diskette: it is faster to keep it in memory and write it away a block at a time. You may, therefore, be switching off before the program has written the last block. There are other reasons, but accept for now that if you have finished working with the program, you use the QUIT command.

Entering data

Before adding data to the file, we have to tell dBase II which of our files we want to use. This may seem confusing when we have only just created the file, but you may recall that the program did ask us whether we wanted to add data immediately after the file was created, and that, in this case, we replied with an 'N'. The program is

Storing Your Data 13

now ready to start work on any file we tell it. We do so by means of the USE command:

. use books (or b:books)

There is no need to supply the full filename: the .DBF suffix will be assumed.

The program will search the diskette for a file called BOOKS.DBF. When it has located the file, the dot prompt will reappear. If the file was not found as a consequence of misspelling, or because we specified the wrong drive, the program will reply with a 'file does not exist' message.

You may want to check the structure of the file. This is done by entering DISPLAY STRUCTURE (or DISP STRU for short) which will present us with the details we entered when the file was created. It will also give one or two other pieces of information such as the number of records on the file. Since we have not yet entered any details of books, the number of records will be given as zero. The dot prompt will, of course, reappear at the end of this information.

Now enter APPEND. The screen will clear, and a formatted data entry screen will appear as follows:

```
TITLE    :                                           :
AUTHOR   :                        :
CLASS    :               :
LOCATION:         :
COST     :    :
```

The field names will be those used when the file was created, which demonstrates how important it is to choose names that are meaningful weeks or months later, or even to other people who might be helping you to add data. The colons show the size of each field: if you enter information past the colon, a beep will sound as a warning and the rest of the data will continue in the next field. You will see shortly how to recover from such an event, but let us first consider what actions are required to enter data.

You should now decide whether you want to keep your data in capitals or in upper- and lower-case, and set the capitals lock on the keyboard accordingly. You will also need to know how to enter a decimal field such as Cost which was defined with a width of 5,2:

Entering 3 will give you 03.00
Entering 34 will give you 34.00
Entering 342, which is larger than 99.99, will give an unusable result

Entering 34.2 will give you 34.20
Entering 34.25 will give you 34.25

If you want to enter a negative amount, simply enter a minus sign followed by the amount. Remember that you should have allowed an extra position at CREATE time if you had anticipated entering negative values.

Now, enter a title, press return; enter the author, press return; enter the classification, press return; enter the location, press return; enter the cost and press return. For example:

```
TITLE    : As You Like It                    :
AUTHOR   : Shakespeare                :
CLASS    : Drama             :
LOCATION: Hall   :
COST     : 3.45 :
```

Before you can blink, the data has been taken, and the screen returns for details of the next book. At the top of the screen, it will tell you the current record number, i.e. how many books you will have entered after this one.

It may be worthwhile pointing out at this stage that you should choose a consistent method of entering the classification and location details. If, afterwards, you want to list all plays, it will not help if you have classified them variously as Drama, Plays, Play, Stage, etc. Nor will you find it easy to put together all the books in the dining-room if you have coded their location as DR, D/R, DINING, etc.

Returning to the entry of data, the program will accept and store data as fast as you can type. (Do not be too concerned with the occasional spelling error: you can always correct it afterwards.) It should also be pointed out here that although this book has taken several pages to cover the stages of creating a file and adding some data, had we been sitting at a keyboard, it would have taken no more than 90 seconds to get this far. In a computer world which is characterised by slow programming and slow development of applications, it is gratifying to be able, in such a short space of time, to create a file and have a ready-made screen provided to take the data we want to add to the file.

After that fanfare, let me sound a word of warning: dBase II can fall prey to outside interference. If someone kicked the mains plug and the computer powered down, all the data entered would not necessarily be sitting safely on the diskette: it is necessary to close a file correctly to ensure that no data is lost. This is because data is

Storing Your Data 15

stored in memory and only written to the diskette at intervals. By closing a file, you write all the details to the diskette. It is tedious, but advisable, to close a file regularly when adding a large number of records. You do this by coming out of the APPEND function (which is done by pressing return at the start of the first field) and, once the dot appears, entering USE BOOKS (or B:BOOKS). That signals the end of work on the file which is then closed down and immediately re-opened. (USE on its own would simply have closed the file down.) Now enter APPEND, and continue adding data.

While in append mode, it is possible to move the cursor backwards and forwards in a field, or up and down from one field to another. The easiest way to slip past a field is to use the return key. If, for example, we do not wish to enter an author for a certain book, say a Dictionary, then simply press return when you reach the Author field. Remember, however, that this would not apply to the very first field which must contain some information. There is a standard diamond of keys which are used in conjunction with the CTRL key to move the cursor about if it becomes necessary to backtrack to correct part of the entry.

CTRL and S moves the cursor to the left.
CTRL and D moves the cursor to the right.
CTRL and E moves the cursor up.
CTRL and X moves the cursor down.

The other cursor control keys are as follows:

CTRL and G deletes characters at the cursor.
CTRL and Y deletes an entire field by setting it to spaces.
CTRL and V switches Insert on and off. Insert allows you to enter extra characters or words into a field by moving the remainder of the characters to the right.

The remaining cursor control keys are CTRL and A, and CTRL and F, which perform functions identical to CTRL and E, and CTRL and X respectively.

Now, say you are about to enter six or seven dramas by Shakespeare, all located in the hall. The only detail which would vary would be the title. Do you want to enter the playwright's name,

16 *Working With dBase II*

the classification and the location seven times or would you rather have it done for you after the first time?

In a situation where much of the details are repeated from one entry to the next, to avoid re-keying the repetitive details you use the SET CARRY ON command. This will leave the previously entered details on the screen even though the screen has changed over ready for the next record. All you need to do is to enter the new title (taking care to remove any unwanted text still remaining from the previous entry), and press return to bypass each of the fields which remain the same.

If the first field is to be repeated, you may not use the return key since on the first field it signals to dBase II that you have finished appending. Instead, you use CTRL and X to move the cursor down one field. You may, of course, use CTRL and X instead of return to bypass the other fields as well. Another cursor control key which may be used to save you pressing return, or CTRL and X, all the way down the list of fields is CTRL and C.

When using SET CARRY ON and entering a numeric field, be careful to get the amount positioned correctly and its decimals in full (even if the right-most decimal is a zero), since any digits remaining from the previous screen would be included in the new amount. For example, if the screen showed 03.48 and you entered 7.5 (which would be quite acceptable on an empty APPEND screen), you would have 07.58 as the result.

The CARRY ON mode remains in force until you QUIT the program or issue the SET CARRY OFF command.

Editing data

If we have now entered the details of all the books in the hall, let us pause and review what we have entered to see if we can spot any obvious mistakes. Press return at the start of the next screen to exit from the APPEND mode, and the prompt dot will appear. Now secure the data you have entered so far by entering USE BOOKS (or B:BOOKS).

Next enter the command EDIT. The program will ask you for the number of the record you want to edit, i.e. change. You may also use this facility simply to inspect the details without changing any of it.

Let us assume for the moment that we have entered a mere thirty books, and that we can afford the time to sit and look at the details of each one in turn. In response to the requests for a record number, we enter 1. Immediately, the familiar data entry screen appears with the record number at the top:

RECORD 00001

```
TITLE    : As You Like It              :
AUTHOR   : Shakespeare                 :
CLASS    : Drama           :
LOCATION: Hall    :
COST     :    3.45:
```

It all looks quite satisfactory, so we press the return key until the screen changes and Record 00002 appears. We can work our way through all 30 records in this way: any changes made on the way will replace the original information. You will find, however, that when you have finished with a record it is faster to move on to the next record by using CTRL and C.

Changes are made by using the cursor control keys described earlier to position the cursor over the data to be changed and inserting, deleting or amending characters as necessary. The following examples will show how this is done:

```
Before:  TITLE    : A Tale of Cities             :
```

Use CTRL and D to move the cursor to the right until it is on the 'C' of 'Cities'. Press CTRL and V to set the insert mode on. Now enter the word 'Two' followed by a space. Press CTRL and V to switch the Insert mode off.

```
After:   TITLE    : A Tale of Two Cities         :

Before:  TITLE    : Treasurer Island             :
```

Use CTRL and D to move the cursor to the right until it is on the spurious 'r' at the end of the first word of the Title. Hold CTRL down and press G once. The 'r' will disappear and the remainder will move left to fill up the vacated position.

```
After:   TITLE    : Treasure Island              :

Before:  TITLE    : Tyrn of the Screw, The       :
```

Use CTRL and D to move the cursor to the 'y' in the first word of the Title. Enter the letter 'u'.

```
After:   TITLE    : Turn of the Screw, The       :
```

A quick method of moving on to the next record during editing is to use CTRL and C. You may also return to an earlier record by using CTRL and R. An unwanted record may be marked for deletion by CTRL and U. A second CTRL and U on the same record will remove the deletion marker. The actual deletion does not take place until other commands which physically delete the record are given. These will be discussed in a later chapter.

Finally, if you do not want to inspect the remaining records on the file, you may exit from the EDIT mode by using CTRL and W (CTRL and O for the Superbrain computer).

The above assumes that we began at the beginning of the file and inspected each record in turn. If, however, we have entered several hundred records, we are unlikely to want to sit patiently at the screen reviewing each record; it would be faster to print all the records together with their record numbers.

We may then check the listing and mark any errors for subsequent correction. The method of listing the records will be discussed shortly: let us assume for now that we have found an error in Record 164. Enter the EDIT command followed by 164: there is no need to wait to be asked for the record number:

```
. EDIT 164

RECORD 00164
TITLE   : Far fom the Madding Crowd            :
AUTHOR  : Hardy, Thomas         :
CLASS   : Novel           :
LOCATION: Hall    :
COST    :  4.50:
```

Use the cursor control keys and the Insert mode to change 'fom' in the Title to 'from'. Then enter CTRL and W, after which the dot prompt will reappear. You may now enter EDIT again followed by the next record number of the next record to be corrected.

In summary, we have so far learned how to create a file, how to add records to the file, and how, afterwards, to correct any mistakes that may have been made when entering the data. In the next chapter we will turn to ways of listing the information.

Chapter Three
Listing Your Data

Listing records

One of the earliest things you will want to do is to see, either on the screen or on paper, what has been entered. There are several means of doing so, but let us consider the simplest method first, the LIST command.

Entering LIST on its own will list every record in full. Fields will appear in the sequence they were specified during the CREATE function, and each field will occupy its maximum number of positions, e.g. 40 for the Title. Each record will be preceded by its record number.

Records which exceed the width of the screen will be folded so that any excess occupies the next line(s) down. If the SET PRINT ON command had been issued previously, the information will also appear on the printer.

The LIST command may be enhanced by adding one or more of the following:

- The fields to be listed.
- Selection criteria.
- Record number suppression.

The fields to be listed
These are supplied in the sequence you want to see them appear (left to right). Fields are separated by commas. For example:

    . list author,title

will produce the following:

        00001 Shakespeare   As You Like It
        00002 Austen,Jane   Pride and Prejudice
        00003 Dickens   Dombey and Son

```
           00004  Stevenson,R L   Treasure Island
           00005  James,Henry     Turn of the Screw
           00006  Hardy,Thomas    Far from the Madding Crowd
           00007  Shakespeare     Henry V
```

Part of a field may be specified by using the Substring function ($), e.g. $(Author,1,5) will list 'Shakespeare' as 'Shake'. The parameters of the Substring function are enclosed in brackets and consist of:

> Fieldname
> Start Position
> Number of Characters

Trailing spaces may be removed from a field by using the TRIM function. For example:

> trim(author)

Any fields to the right will be shifted to the left by the number of spaces that are trimmed. Constants may be introduced by enclosing them in double quotes. For example:

```
    . list trim(author),":",title
    00001  Shakespeare : As You Like It
    00002  Austen,Jane : Pride and Prejudice
    00003  Dickens : Dombey and Son
    00004  Stevenson,R L : Treasure Island
    00005  James,Henry : Turn of the Screw
    00006  Hardy,Thomas : Far from the Madding Crowd
```

The selection criteria

These allow you to specify which records you want to include in your list (all others will be ignored). For example, to select only books by Dickens you would enter the following:

> . list for author="Dickens"

Note, however, that you have to provide the correct combination of upper- and lower-case: "Dickens" will not find entries which contain "DICKENS". Later you will be shown how to get around this restriction, but for now we will simply be consistent in entering and using information. "Dickens" will always be that and not "dickens" or "DICKENS" (unless, of course, you elected at the beginning to work in upper-case throughout).

The quotation marks are required by dBase II when you are working with a field described at the CREATE stage as a character field. A field which had been described as numeric would not require them.

The selection criteria may be quite complex, and cover more than one field. For example:

. list for author="Wilde" .and. class="Poems" .and.;
location="Lounge"

Comparison operators are as follows:

    =   equal
    #   not equal (<> is an alternative)
    <   less than
    >   greater than
    <=   less than or equal
    >=   greater than or equal
    $ equal or contained in (e.g. "We"$author will select Wells, H.G. and West, Morris)

A selection based on two or more conditions is specified by using logical operations:

.AND.   eg. author="Hardy" .and. class="Novel"

.OR.   eg. class="Drama" .or. class="Poetry"

.NOT.   eg. .not. location="Hall"

The .NOT. operator is very useful for applying an exclusion. For example:

. list for .not.(author="Dickens" .and. location="Hall")

This means list everything but Dickens books in the hall.

Record number suppression

You may prevent the record numbers appearing by entering OFF as the last part of the LIST command. For example:

  . list author,title for class="Drama" off
  Shakespeare   As You Like It
  Shakespeare   Henry V

There is another dBase II command which is very similar to the LIST command. This is the DISPLAY command. The two commands are identical in all but three respects:

(1) DISPLAY allows you to specify the number of records you want to see, e.g. NEXT 5, while LIST processes all the records on the file. On its own, DISPLAY will produce just one record.

(2) LIST will always start at the beginning of the file, while DISPLAY will start at the current record. Thus, GOTO 7 followed by DISPLAY will show record 00007.

(3) LIST will show all the records on the file without interruption. DISPLAY will show 15 records and wait for you to press any key before it shows the next 15 records.

Other than in respect of the above, you may consider LIST and DISPLAY interchangeable.

The initial reaction to the LIST command is one of pleased surprise that it is so easy to select and print the contents of your database. Soon, however, you notice that it does not stop at the end of the page: it just carries on printing over the perforations separating pages. Nor does it allow you to provide headings, dates, page numbers or, in a financial application, sub-totals, totals, etc. All of these are available with another method of presenting information which will be explained next.

Creating a report

The REPORT command improves on the facilities of DISPLAY and LIST by adding page headings, field headings, totalling and sub-totalling, summary reporting, and a certain amount of control over the page lay-out.

The REPORT command employs a question-and-answer technique to obtain much of the details such as the page heading, totalling requirements, etc. However, some of the information is supplied as part of the command (as with the LIST command), and we will cover these first:

(1) Since you are unlikely to want to type in all the page headings and other details every time you want to run the report, you may give it a name which dBase II will use to create a special file to contain all these details. In the example below, we have decided to call the report ALLBOOK:

```
. report form allbook (or b:allbook)
```

Following the question-and-answer procedure (which will be explained shortly), the report details are written to a file called ALLBOOK.FRM. When you enter the same command next time, the program will take the word following the keyword FORM, add the standard suffix .FRM to it, and try to find a file with that name. If it succeeds, it will use the information contained in the file to produce the report. If it cannot find the file, it will assume that you want to create a new Report file and start the question-and-answer procedure.

(2) The number of records you want to see, e.g. NEXT 5, may be specified. If this is not specified, the program assumes that all the records on the database are to be shown.

(3) You may provide selection criteria. For example:

. Report form novels for class = "Novel"

(4) You may send your report to the printer by adding TO PRINT

. Report form allbook to print

(5) You may suppress the page number and date headings which would otherwise appear at the top of each page by adding PLAIN to the command line.

Once you have completed the command line, the program will ask you for further information. The following is a simple example:

```
. report form allbook
ENTER OPTIONS, M=LEFT MARGIN, L=LINES/PAGE, W=PAGE WIDTH w=65
PAGE HEADING? (Y/N) y
ENTER PAGE HEADING: Complete List of Books
DOUBLE SPACE REPORT? (Y/N) n
ARE TOTALS REQUIRED? (Y/N) n
COL     WIDTH,CONTENTS
001     25,author
ENTER HEADING: <Author;------
002     40,title
ENTER HEADING: <Title;-----
003     <CR>
```

The report the above might produce would look as follows:

```
PAGE NO. 00001

                  Complete List of Books

   Author                  Title
   ------                  -----

   Shakespeare             As You Like It
   Austen,Jane             Pride and Prejudice
   Dickens                 Dombey and Son
   Stevenson,R L           Treasure Island
   James,Henry             Turn of the Screw
   Hardy,Thomas            Far from the Madding Crowd
   Jones,T B               Islands of Greece,The
```

```
Hall,F J              Devon and Cornwall
Jones,Belinda         Microwave Cookery
Anderson,K L          Indian Dishes
Delderfield,R F       Kings and Queens of England
Finberg,H P R         Formation of England,The
Shakespeare           Henry V
Chaucer               Canterbury Tales
Tolstoy               War and Peace
Dickens               Bleak House
Dostoievsky           Crime and Punishment
```

One or two of the conventions will need an explanation so let us go through some of the questions in detail:

(1) *ENTER OPTIONS*
You supply information only if you want to. The program will make assumptions, i.e. use defaults, if you simply press the return key.

M = LEFT MARGIN: This allows you to indent the whole report by the number of spaces you give to M, e.g. M = 20 will leave a left margin of 20 spaces. The default is 8 spaces.

L = LINES/PAGE: This option specifies the number of lines per page. The default is 57. The number of lines include the page headings, so allow for these. Do not be surprised if you try the report out on the screen only (i.e. without specifying TO PRINT) and you do not see the page heading again after the first page; the number of lines per page are only taken into consideration when the program knows that it is sending the report to a printer.

W = PAGE WIDTH: This is only to centre the page heading. The default is 80 characters, i.e. a page heading of 20 characters would begin 30 characters from the left margin. A practical rule would be to make W equal to the sum of the widths of the columns being printed.

(2) *PAGE HEADING*
The program will only ask you for a page heading if you reply 'Y' to this question. When you do enter a heading, type it exactly as you want to see it, i.e. with upper- and lower-case, or all upper-case. If you want to underline it, follow the last letter of the heading with a semi-colon, and then enter as many underline characters, e.g. =, * or −, as you want – usually as many as the heading is long.

(3) *ARE TOTALS REQUIRED?*
If you reply 'Y' to this, the program will next ask you whether you want sub-totals. If you reply 'Y' again, it will ask you for the name of the field on which to sub-total, so that every time the contents of that field changes a sub-total can be thrown out. Totals, of course, only

appear at the very end of the report. Also, if you asked for subtotalling, the program will enquire whether you want to have a summary report only, i.e. show only the sub-totals against the subtotal field without showing the individual records which make up the sub-total. Later when you are entering the field names, if the field is one which has been described during the CREATE stage as numeric, the program will ask you whether totals are required for that field.

You may also provide a heading for the sub-total which will be shown beside the sub-total field at the start of each set of lines preceding the sub-total. In addition, you will be asked whether you want the printer to throw to a new page after printing a sub-total.

You are, by now, probably wondering how it is possible to provide sub-totalling on information which is not in any special sequence. When you discover that the REPORT command does not provide a sorting facility, you will be even more puzzled. The answer lies in the fact that you would use this command on a file that has been indexed or sorted previously. Either is very simple to do and requires hardly any effort on your part; both are explained in Chapter 4.

(4) *COL WIDTH, CONTENTS*

The program supplies each column number automatically as a prompt. We are required to supply the number of positions we want our information to occupy, and a description of the information which is to be placed there.

Typically, the contents of a column would be specified by supplying a fieldname. It is, however, possible to specify contents which are derived from database fields, particularly in financial applications. For example, the sum of the fields contained in two earlier columns, or an earlier field multiplied by a constant exchange or inflation rate may be specified. If you supply the name of a field which is not defined in the database in use, you will be asked to re-enter the line.

After the width and contents of a report column has been supplied, you are invited to provide a column heading. As with the page heading, you may enter underlining characters. You may also specify left or right justification of the heading by preceding the column heading with a $<$ or $>$ respectively. For example:

    $<$ Author

In the absence of either of these the column heading will be centralised.

26 *Working With dBase II*

If you had replied 'Y' to the ARE TOTALS REQUIRED? question, and if the field is numeric, you will now be asked whether you want to total the column.

When you have described each column of the report, you signal to dBase II that you have completed your entries by pressing the return key when the next column number prompt appears. The program will then write your report definition to a file and immediately proceed to produce the report.

Page numbers are automatically supplied. You may also include a date by issuing the SET DATE TO command prior to the REPORT command. For example:

```
. set date to 06/06/84
```

The SET DATE TO command must, however, be given each time; it is not stored with the rest of the report details. Similarly, an additional heading may be entered at run time with the command SET HEADING TO. For example:

```
. set heading to Special List for School
```

The above command would print the run time heading beside the page number each time you produce the report, until you reissue the command with a different run time heading or QUIT the program.

You may, of course, be wondering how you change the REPORT details which have been written to the .FRM file without having to go through the entire question-and-answer procedure a second time. If you look at the .FRM file with a word processor or the dBase II MODIFY COMMAND statement, you will see that the REPORT details are stored line by line much as you entered them. It is a simple matter to change a heading or totalling requirement and save the amended file when you have finished. The MODIFY COMMAND command is explained in Chapter 7, but in this context remember that when you use this command to amend .FRM files you must supply the full filename. For example:

```
. modify command allbook.frm
```

You may use the cursor controls described in the section on editing in Chapter 2 to make your changes. When you have completed the changes, use CTRL and W to save the .FRM file.

Locating files

If you have loaded dBase II from the A: drive, unless you stipulate otherwise, the A: drive will be expected to contain all files. (The converse is true if you loaded the program from the B: drive.) We have already created two types of file – the .DBF or Database itself, and the .FRM or Report Form file. Now we are about to create others, so it is time to explain how to avoid entering the B: in front of any file located on the diskette in the second drive.

There are a great many SET commands (all of which will be covered as we progress) and one of these allows you to tell dBase II that until you change the drive again or quit the program, it should search for files on the drive you specify:

. set default to b:

Remember, though, that while you no longer have to prefix files on the B: drive with B:, you now have to supply the A: prefix for any files you want on that drive. Also, if you want only your database on the B: drive for reasons of space, then it is better not to set the B: drive as the default. This is because you are bound to forget to provide the A: prefix for some of the Report Form or other incidental files which you will want to create to process your database.

If you want to find out which files are on which drive, you can do so without leaving dBase II by using the DISPLAY FILES (or LIST FILES) command. If you do not supply any of the parameters, only files with the .DBF suffix will be listed. You may, therefore, extend the command as follows:

.display files like *.frm

or

.display files like *.*

The latter will display all files on the current drive. If you want to list the files on the other drive, you add a further parameter:

display files like *.* on b:

or

display files like *.* on a:

Chapter Four
Working With Your Data

Getting the data into sequence

Although it is convenient to enter information in no particular order, we do need the data in some sort of sequence when we want to list it – such as, for example, titles by author listed alphabetically.

There are two methods which may be used to achieve a particular sequence: one is indexing, and the other sorting. The difference lies in speed, the size of the resulting file, whether or not the sequence is automatically maintained afterwards when you update the file, and the number of fields that may be used to sequence the information. Indexing operates on one or more selected fields and creates an index file which contains pointers to the records in the database. Sorting operates on a single field only and recreates the database in full, but in the requested sequence. Indexing is faster when you create the index but can be slower to use, for example when the entire database is listed, because the information is being accessed randomly. Sorting takes longer to do, but afterwards all the information is available in the desired sequence by changing your USE to the sorted file. A major plus on the side of indexing is that it is able to update the index automatically when you update a file which has been indexed. Indexing and sorting both specify the field(s) which control the sequencing, and the name of the file which is to contain the end result.

Indexing
The following is an example of the INDEX command:

. Index on author to authind

or

. Index on location to locind

Working With Your Data 29

The program will write the index to the filename you specified and add the suffix .NDX. For example:

AUTHIND.NDX

or

LOCIND.NDX

When you have indexed a file, and until you change your use of the file, reset the index, or exit the program, access to the file or listing it will be in the indexed sequence. To employ the same sequence on a subsequent occasion, you have to provide the name of the indexed file when you open a database. For example:

. use books index authind

The following serves to illustrate the difference:

- Without indexing:

        . use books
        . list author
        00001   Shakespeare
        00002   Austen,Jane
        00003   Dickens
        00004   Stevenson,R L
        00005   James,Henry
        00006   Hardy,Thomas

- With indexing:

        . use books index authind
        . list author
        00002   Austen,Jane
        00003   Dickens
        00006   Hardy,Thomas
        00005   James,Henry
        00001   Shakespeare
        00004   Stevenson,R L

The indexing sequence may be ascending or descending. Descending sequence is obtained by prefixing the fieldname with a minus sign, thus:

        . use books
        . index on −author to authind
        . list author
        00004   Stevenson,R L
        00001   Shakespeare

```
     00005   James,Henry
     00006   Hardy,Thomas
     00003   Dickens
     00002   Austen,Jane
```

Descending sequence will be particularly useful for numeric fields, say to rank items on a cost basis.

More than one field, and even parts of a field, may be used to create an index. Fields are joined with the + operator. For example:

```
. index on class+author to classind
```

A part of a character field may be selected with the Substring function ($), thus:

```
. index on author+$(title,1,15) to bookind
```

A part of a numeric field may be used as an index field if the field is converted to character format with the String function (STR). The parameters of this function are:

Field
Length
Number of decimal places

The following will index on the integer part of Cost:

```
. index on str(cost,2,0) to costind
```

You may index a file more than once and specify different indexes when using a file depending on the sequence required. Consider, however, that you may be updating the file. How do you ensure that additions or changes are included in the index? The answer lies in remembering to supply the name of the indexed file each time you perform an update. For example,

```
. use books index bookind
. append
```

will update the BOOKIND.NDX file with every addition to the BOOKS.DBF file.

If you are maintaining more than one index – say, an author index and a location index – you specify the names of both indexes in the USE statement:

```
. use books index authind,locind
```

This may seem strange since one would not expect to use a file in more than one sequence at the same time, i.e. strict author sequence could conflict with location sequence. However, ony the first named index will dictate the sequence of the file. The remainder are concerned only with automatic updating. Up to seven indexes may be specified in a USE command and all will be updated automatically when you add or change records.

You may, also, bring an index into use with the SET INDEX TO command. The SET INDEX TO command could, for example, switch you to an alternative index or indexes. It does, however, cancel any existing indexes so you should include these in the list if you want them to continue. For example:

```
.set index to authind,locind,bookind
```

Version 2.4 of dBase II has a new command which you will find invaluable in keeping track of the indexes you have set up. This is the DISPLAY STATUS command which displays the files that are in USE plus any index files which have been named in the USE or SET INDEX TO commands. The command is particularly useful in reminding you of the fields that you used when you created the index.

You should remember to maintain your index files when using any of the following commands:

APPEND
EDIT
REPLACE
BROWSE
CHANGE
PACK

REPLACE, BROWSE, and CHANGE are commands that are similar to EDIT in effect, i.e. in changing the contents of fields. If either EDIT, REPLACE, BROWSE, or CHANGE have changed the contents of fields which had been used for indexing purposes, it will obviously be necessary to apply these changes to the index file(s). With one exception, you do this simply by remembering to specify the indexes as described above. The exception is the CHANGE command. If you have used this command to change fields which control indexing, you have to set the index(es) up from scratch.

PACK physically removes records which have earlier been marked for deletion and you should therefore ensure that the index files reflect these deletions and the new positions of subsequent records. Unfortunately, PACK will only adjust one index file. You have to see to any remaining ones yourself by setting them up a second time.

Sorting
Sorting creates a copy of the database in the required sort sequence, i.e. the resulting file takes up as much space as the original. Another point to bear in mind is that having sorted a file, the resulting file is not maintained, i.e. updated with additions or changes. If you want an up-to-date sorted version, you have to execute the SORT command again. The advantage of a sorted file is that it is faster to list (in the sorted sequence) than an indexed file.

The command is as follows:

    . sort on author to booksrt

The resulting file will be called BOOKSRT.DBF. You may have as many sorted versions of your database as you wish, but remember that you are likely to run into space problems.

The SORT command is less flexible than INDEX since it will accept a single field only. Nor will it accept part of a field, i.e. you cannot use the Substring function.

It is possible to sort the BOOKS file into, say, Titles alphabetically within Authors alphabetically by performing two separate sorts. First you sort on the minor of the two fields, i.e. Titles. This is followed by a sort which sorts on the major field, i.e. Author. You could continue sorting, always from minor to major, until you run out of fields and finish up with a totally structured database.

You may specify ascending or descending sequence: the former will be assumed if you do not specify either. Descending sequence is specified by including the word DESCENDING as part of the command, not by prefixing the fieldname with a minus sign as with the INDEX command.

In sorting (and indexing for that matter), lower-case letters sort after upper-case letters. Thus, if you had inadvertently entered an author, say 'Balzac', completely in lower-case, and then sorted on Authors, you would find that author at the end. For example:

    Dickens
    Joyce, James
    Shakespeare
    Tolstoy
    balzac

If you do need to maintain a strict alphabetic sequence

irrespective of upper- or lower-case, you may do your indexing as follows:

. index on !(author) to authind

The ! function converts all lower-case letters to upper-case. In this example, all the index entries will be in upper-case, and thus in strict alphabetical sequence, but the details on the file will remain as you entered them.

The SORT command will not accept the ! function, but there is another way of creating a sorted file. It consists of using the dBase II COPY command on a file that is already indexed. For example:

. use books index authind
. copy to booksrt

The COPY command will create a new database file with the name BOOKSRT and copy all the records from BOOKS into the new file. It will, however, copy the records in the indexed sequence so that you finish up with a sorted file. Your index may, of course, be one that you set up with the ! function.

Generally, you will find indexing to be more convenient than sorting. There could, however, be a case for using SORT where you have set up a database which changes rarely, and where you want to produce listings quickly in a fixed sequence.

Working at the screen

As you have no doubt already discovered in the course of using the EDIT command, dBase II uses the position of a record in the file, i.e. the record number, as a means of keeping track of records. Thus Record Number 00003 is the third record in the file. Unless a file is sorted, or records are deleted by using the PACK command or inserted with the INSERT command, a particular record number will always identify the same record.

When you open an existing file (without specifying an index) with the USE command, you are positioned at record 00001. By using the DISPLAY command on its own, i.e. without parameters, you will be able to look at the contents of this record. Remember that DISPLAY used in this way will show you the current record only: at this moment, the current record is 00001. Now enter the command SKIP. This moves you on one record. If you repeat the DISPLAY command, you will see that the current record is now record 00002.

You may SKIP in either direction and for more than one record. For example:

```
. skip -2
. skip 15
```

Now enter GO 5 or GOTO 5. This time DISPLAY will give you record 00005 as the current record number. Variations on GOTO 5 are GOTO RECORD 5, or even just 5. Other methods of moving about in the file are given below, but remember that none of these will do more than get you to a particular record: you have to provide an additional command, e.g. DISPLAY, to look at the record details.

- GO (or GOTO) BOTTOM will take you to the last record on the file.
- GO (or GOTO) TOP will take you to the first record on the file.
- LOCATE will search the file for a specified item. For example:

```
. locate for author="Dickens"
```

- FIND will search for a specified item that has been indexed. For example:

```
. find Dickens
```

LOCATE

LOCATE reads through the file, stops when it has found the first record which corresponds to the specified criteria, and displays its record number. When you have inspected the record, you may resume the search by using the CONTINUE command. If the criteria are not satisfied, an end-of-file message will be displayed or, if you limited the search by using the NEXT clause, e.g. NEXT 15, an end-of-locate message will be displayed. For example:

```
. locate next 20 for class="Travel"
END OF LOCATE
```

If you use the NEXT clause, LOCATE will commence the search at the current record. Otherwise it will read through the file from the beginning. If you specified an index with the USE command, the file will be read in indexed sequence which could be slower.

The substring operator ($) may be used to some advantage with the LOCATE command. It is used as A $ B to see if A is equal to or contained in B. For example:

```
. locate for "Madding"$title
```

```
RECORD: 00021
. disp title
00021 Far From the Madding Crowd
```

Note that we were looking for a word contained in the Title, so that word had to appear to the left of the substring operator.

LOCATE is useful for ad hoc enquiries without regard for the sequence of a file. Any of the comparison operators described under the LIST and DISPLAY commands may be used.

FIND

FIND will also search for specified criteria, but operates on an index file instead of the database itself. It is therefore a prerequisite to using the FIND command that an index file has been opened:

```
. use books index locind
. find H
. display location
00071 Hall
```

The above illustrates how you are able to position yourself to, say, the first book located in the hall. Note that you do not need to supply the quotation marks usually required when dealing with character fields. Nor do you need to provide more characters than are necessary to reach the required record. For example:

```
. use books index authind
. find W
. display author
00046 Wallace, Edgar
. find Wi
. display author
00073 Wilde, Oscar
```

You are not able to move the current record pointer on one record and try again, because FIND always begins its search from the beginning of the index, however many times you repeat it. The fact that FIND operates on an index makes it very fast and you will discover that it will position you as requested within seconds. If you had previously issued the SET DELETED ON command, FIND will ignore records which have been marked for deletion.

Since you are using the command with an index, you may follow it with other commands such as SKIP to present you with the next record in sequence. You may even use the LOCATE command which, provided you specify the NEXT clause, will start at the current record, i.e. the one you obtained with FIND. This presents you with only those records which match your requirements. For example:

```
. find Smith
. display author,title
00114 Smith,A E                     Riding the Range
. locate next 999 for "Smith"$author
RECORD 00114
. continue
RECORD 00115
. display author,title
00115 Smith,T                       Keep Fit with Yoga
. continue
END OF FILE
```

NEXT 999 is simply a way of specifying a large number of records starting with the current record. Although you had already 'located' the first Smith with the FIND command, and the LOCATE command found it again, LOCATE was used to set you up for the CONTINUE commands. You could alternatively have displayed the result of the FIND command, and then used the SKIP command to move on to the next record before issuing the LOCATE.

Now that we have discussed how to position the current record pointer to the first of a set of records which match a specific condition, we are going to look at a smaller number of commands which will operate only while the condition remains true. Some of these you have already met – LIST or DISPLAY, and REPORT. The new element is the WHILE clause. For example:

```
. list author, title while location="Hall"
```

This may not seem very different to using the FOR clause, until you realise that the command has been speeded up significantly. If you had used FOR, the command would have read through the file from start to end looking for records which match the condition. The WHILE clause starts executing the command at the current record and will stop it as soon as the condition is no longer true. If the current record does not meet the condition, the command will not operate at all.

WHILE will be found as an option in most commands which contain the FOR clause (the two clauses are mutually exclusive):

DISPLAY
LIST
REPORT

COUNT
SUM
TOTAL
DELETE
RECALL
REPLACE
COPY TO
APPEND FROM

Other than the first three which have already been discussed, these commands will shortly be covered in detail, but to avoid repetition, the WHILE clause will not be explained each time; when you see the FOR clause just remember the WHILE alternative.

Counting and totalling

If we want to find out how many records there are on the database, we could do so by entering DISPLAY STRUCTURE (or DISP STRU). The dBase II response would contain the number of records as well as a description of the file structure. If, however, we wanted to know how many records there were in a particular category, we would need a more precise means of counting. The COUNT command allows you to specify the conditions under which records are to be included in the count. For example:

```
.use books
.count for location="Hall"
COUNT = 00097
.count for class="Travel"
COUNT = 00014
```

COUNT has a 'scope' clause, e.g. ALL or NEXT 12, which means that if the NEXT clause had been specified, it would start at the current record and not at the beginning of the file. Records which have been marked for deletion will also be counted but you may ignore them by issuing the SET DELETED ON command.

You may also store the result of the count operation in a temporary field which dBase II makes available to you. The program allows 64 of these temporary fields (or Memory Variables as they are correctly called) and will allocate them as and when you use them:

```
.use books
.count for location="Hall" to Halltotal
COUNT = 00097
.count for location="Study" to Studytot
COUNT = 00046
```

Now that you have been allocated two new field names – Halltotal and Studytot – you may use them as you would any other field: their contents may be added together, multiplied, subtracted, etc. The dBase II command for examining the contents of such a temporary field is '?'. For example:

```
. ? halltotal
    97
. ? studytot
    46
. ? halltotal + studytot
   143
```

Another way to examine the contents of these temporary fields, or memory variables, is to use the DISPLAY MEMORY command:

```
.display memory
HALLTOTAL        (N)         97
STUDYTOT         (N)         46
** TOTAL **      02 VARIABLES USED 00012 BYTES USED
```

As you can see, the display consists of the memory variable name, field-type, e.g. (N) for numeric, and content of each memory variable. Remember though that they are temporary fields: the next time you switch on, dBase II will not recognise those field names unless you repeat the previous procedure of using them to hold data.

A command similar in operation to COUNT, but different in purpose, is SUM which will provide totals for specified fields:

```
.use books
.sum cost for class="Travel"
48.72
```

The SUM command will quite happily deal with negative fields, i.e. numeric fields where the value is preceded by a minus sign. Up to five fields may be totalled at once by separating the fieldnames with commas as for the LIST command. The command will operate only on numeric fields, and will ignore records marked for deletion.

The SUM command is quite powerful in that it also allows you to generate totals for combinations of fields, e.g. the sum of two fields multiplied. If our BOOKS database had an extra field showing the number of copies we owned of each book, we could enter the following to find out the total cost of our book collection:

```
.use books
.sum cost*nobooks
132.94
```

You may also combine the SUM and COUNT commands to arrive at an average. For example:

```
.use books
.count for class="Travel" to trcount
COUNT = 00014
.sum cost for class="Travel" to trsum
48.72
? trsum/trcount
        3.48
```

Now you know that your 14 travel books cost you an average of 3.48 per book.

There is a third method of summarising all or part of a file: using the TOTAL command. The word TOTAL is slightly confusing since one expects something along the lines of the operation already described under the SUM command. TOTAL actually creates a second database, which is probably not what you would have expected. The command is used to provide a sub-set of your database containing sub-total records only. In the sequence below, for example, a second database called CLASSTOT would be created containing one record for each classification, e.g. Travel, Cookery, Drama, etc.

```
.use books index classind
.total on class to classfile
00034 RECORDS COPIED
```

The new file, CLASSFILE, would, for example, contain a single record for classification 'Travel' which would show a cost of 48.72, i.e. the total cost for that classification. TOTAL will sub-total every numeric field, i.e. described as Numeric, and write a sub-total record to the new file. You may apply selection criteria by using the FOR clause so that only records which meet the specified condition(s) are sub-totalled. You may also restrict the contents of the individual records on the file by specifying which fields are to be included in the new file. Obviously, any data which are extraneous to the sub-totalling but are allocated fields (in this case author, title, location), would be meaningless. They would simply contain author, title and location details of the first record in each group of classification records. Thus, if the first Travel book in the indexed sequence was 'Exploring India' by F. J. Hall, you would find those details contained in the Travel record on the new file.

You should also beware of overflow on the numeric fields which are being totalled. A numeric field on the new file will be equal in size to that on the original file. Addition may produce an amount which will not fit into that field size. For example, 104.50 will not fit into a field which had been defined as 5,2. (Remember the full stop takes up one of the characters.) The possible future use of the TOTAL command should thus be taken into consideration when designing the file. If you are already finding yourself in that situation, do not despair. You will discover, in Chapter 5, how to change the size of fields in a database which is already in existence.

Review

Let me remind you that we are still skating on the surface of the dBase II facilities. Starting with the CREATE command, we have so far covered no more than twenty-five commands, and there are nearly twice that number more. Yet, we have the following impressive list of tasks:

- Create a database
- Add records
- Change records
- List records
- Create reports
- Provide and maintain indexes
- Sort the database
- Set up enquiry facilities
- Provide ad hoc totalling and sub-totalling

It adds up to what would be quite a large system if you were to program it using COBOL, BASIC, or one of the other standard programming languages. In Part 2, you will discover several other commands including some very useful extra editing commands, how to change the database to add extra fields or change existing ones, and how to use more than one database at the same time.

Part 2
Additional dBase II Techniques

Chapter Five
Changing Your Mind

Inserting records

Insertion presupposes that a file is in a particular sequence, say author sequence, and that when adding a new record it is important to position the new record so that it falls into place in respect to other records. Otherwise one might as well add the record at the end using the APPEND command.

dBase II records are stored as they are entered, that is, in no particular sequence. They may be retrieved or listed in a specific sequence by using the INDEX command or the file may be sorted into a particular sequence (see Chapter 4 for both of these). Given these facilities, the INSERT command is of limited use. It is also quite slow since each time a record is inserted, the entire file is moved on one record. However, there may be occasions when it will be more convenient to insert than, say, to re-sort, particularly where the insertion is close to the end of the file or on a small file. An important point to bear in mind is that if the file is being used with an index, the INSERT command will perform an APPEND, i.e. write the record at the end of the file and simply update the index file to obtain the necessary sequence.

To use INSERT, the program must be directed to the record before or after the place the insertion is to occur. The GOTO command may be used to do this. INSERT on its own will insert the new record after the current record, that is after the one to which we pointed with the GOTO command. INSERT BEFORE will insert the new record in front of the current record.

Having identified where to make the insertion, the program will display the data entry screen just as it did in APPEND. Once the data has been entered, the process of moving records along will commence and eventually the dot prompt will reappear.

It is also possible to ask for a blank record to be inserted by specifying INSERT BLANK or INSERT BEFORE BLANK. In this case, the data entry screen will not be displayed and the program will immediately start moving records.

Let us look at an example:

```
. use books
. list author
00001    Austen,Jane
00002    Balzac
00003    Dickens
00004    Fitzgerald,F.Scott
00005    Shakespeare
```

We now want to insert a record for James Joyce:

```
. goto 4
. insert
```

```
RECORD 00005
TITLE     : Ulysses                              :
AUTHOR    : Joyce,James             :
CLASS     : Novel                   :
LOCATION: Hall    :
COST      : 09.80:
```

The file will now appear as follows:

```
. list author
00001       Austen,Jane
00002       Balzac
00003       Dickens
00004       Fitzgerald,F.Scott
00005       Joyce,James
00006       Shakespeare
```

Deleting records

You have already discovered how to delete a record during the EDIT process by means of CTRL and U. That, however, operates on single records and you may wish for a more powerful method, such as one which deletes all records answering to a specific condition. The DELETE command allows you to specify a condition and then searches as many records as you have specified for those which contain the condition. For example:

```
. delete all for author="Dickens"
```

The above will search the whole file and every record which contains Dickens will be marked for deletion. If ALL had not been specified, only the current record would have been examined. An alternative would be to specify a number of records to be searched (starting with the current record), or indicate a specific record by providing its record number. Examples of these are:

- delete next 20
- delete next 20 for author = "Dickens"
- delete record 93

Deleted records will appear if listed, but will be marked with an asterisk beside the record number. This applies equally to those deleted with the DELETE command and those deleted with CTRL and U during the EDIT procedure. The asterisk will not appear, however, for formatted reports such as those produced by the REPORT command or those which you will encounter in the chapters on programming in Part 3. Before discussing the permanent removal of deleted records, let us consider how to undo a deletion. In the EDIT procedure, you were able to use CTRL and U a second time to unset the deletion marker. Similarly, if you now enter the EDIT command and specify the record number of a record which had been deleted previously (by either means), you may use CTRL and U to undo the deletion.

Here, again, it may be desirable to operate on the whole file and to undo a deletion on all records answering to a given condition, i.e. the exact opposite of the DELETE command. This service is provided by the RECALL command. It operates in precisely the same way as DELETE. You may RECALL ALL, i.e. undo all deletions, specify a record number, or specify a given number of records to be recalled starting at the current record. Or you may specify that all records answering a condition should be recalled. For example:

- recall all for author="Dickens"

Let us now, at last, physically delete the records we have marked for deletion. We are confident that they may be physically removed because we have checked them, and have listed all the records for a really close examination. There are two methods of physically deleting records. The recommended method (given that you have adequate disk space) is to COPY the database:

- use books
- copy to bookscpy

46 Working With dBase II

The COPY command will overwrite an existing file if there is one with the specified filename, in this case BOOKSCPY, or it will create BOOKSCPY if it does not already exist. The copied file will not contain the records which have been tagged for deletion. You may then carry out further reconciliations and checks on the new database without having lost the original which will, of course, still contain all deleted records.

You could, for example, use the COUNT and SUM commands described in Chapter 4. The COUNT command could be used to check that the copied database contains the expected number of records. To count the number of records that have not been deleted on the original database, i.e. the number you expect to copy, use:

```
. count for .not. *
```

SUM could be used to obtain hash totals on both files and agree these. Hash total is a term that refers to a total on any numeric field that is used purely as a control check.

```
. use books
. sum cost
435.98

. use bookscpy
.sum cost
435.98
```

DELETE FILE

Having assured yourself that all is well, you may use another feature of the DELETE command, that is DELETE FILE:

```
.delete file books
```

Some prudent users may even have copied the old database to a spare diskette before using the DELETE FILE command. You may carry out the copy and/or delete file functions in dBase II as already explained, or revert to the CP/M or DOS operating system to do so. Similarly, you may use dBase II or CP/M, etc., to change the name of the new database back to that of the original (after you have deleted the original). In dBase II you use the RENAME command:

RENAME

```
. rename bookscpy to books
```

The second method of physically deleting records is that of the PACK command. This method consists, as the name indicates, of repacking the records in situ. There is no going back. Once you have started the PACK operation, the records marked for deletion are lost permanently. More important, if someone should kick the mains supply or the computer is powered down for any reason, you will have a messy and, in most cases, unusable database on your hands. There are times, however, when diskette space constraints will render this the only method available to you. In such cases, use the operating system commands to secure your file to a back-up copy before going into dBase II to do the PACK operation.

There is another consideration to using the PACK command which may persuade you in its favour. If you PACK a file which is indexed and you specified the index in the USE command prior to the PACK, the index file will be adjusted by the PACK command. Unfortunately, only one such index will be updated automatically.

More editing

Apart from the method discussed in Chapter 2, there are three other methods of editing. The first is REPLACE which may be used to edit all or some of the records in a file at a single sweep. The example below will replace consistent misspellings of an author's name with the correct version wherever the misspelling should occur:

```
.replace all author with "Dickens" for author="Dikens"
00004 REPLACEMENT(S)
```

If the scope of the command, e.g. ALL, is not specified, REPLACE will act only on the current record. Take care, however, because if you use the FOR clause, the default is ALL and not current record. As an alternative, you could specify a number of records to be searched (starting with the current record), or indicate a specific record to be searched by providing its record number. For example:

```
.replace next 20 author with "Marx" for author="Max"
```

```
.replace record 114 author with "Marx" for author="Max"
```

More than one replacement may be requested in a single command. For example:

```
.replace all author with "Dickens",class with "Novel";
             for author="Dikens"
```

REPLACE is particularly useful when it becomes necessary to change your classification of certain records. Say you wanted to introduce a new category of books called "Computer, Personal" or "Computer,P.C." but that, hitherto, you had entered all books on the subject of computers simply as "Computer". You could, of course, have a section of books classified under "Computer" and another under "Computer,P.C.", but let us accept that you would prefer to have a correct description in each case, and that it will be necessary to change "Computer" to "Computer,M.F." to describe mainframe computers. You would then do the following:

```
.replace all class with "Computer,M.F." for class=;
   "Computer"
```

Or you may realise that you have some books already entered under the classification of "Computer" which deal with Personal Computers, and that they are all located in the lounge. You would then issue the following command:

```
.replace all class with "Computer,M.F." for class=;
   "Computer" .and. location#"Lounge"
```

Any tidying up of individual cases may be performed with the EDIT command, or with one of the following two commands:

> CHANGE
> BROWSE

CHANGE is similar to REPLACE in that you may specify which records (i.e. ALL, NEXT 20, etc.) and which conditions are to be met, e.g. FOR AUTHOR="Dickens", but it requires you to change each record yourself. Only those records which meet the specified conditions are presented to you (and you may request that only certain fields are presented), but you are nevertheless making every change yourself. The following illustrates the procedure:

```
.change all field author for author="Dikens"
RECORD 00019
AUTHOR: Dikens
CHANGE? k
TO      ck
AUTHOR: Dickens
CHANGE?
```

As you can see, after you have made your change the field is re-presented for you to check and correct if necessary. If you now press return, the next record which meets the specified condition will be presented. To exit from the CHANGE procedure before all requested records have been presented, press the escape key.

BROWSE is equivalent to EDIT but has no parameters. It starts at the current record and, provided that no field is greater than 80 characters, presents you with 19 records. Each record occupies one line (again provided a field does not exceed 80 characters) and as many complete fields as may be contained in the screen width will be shown. You will shortly see how to get at the remaining fields. For the moment, it is important to realise that in BROWSE you have an EDIT command which allows you to look at and edit up to 19 records at a time. Many of the same rules apply:

CTRL and E or A moves the cursor to the previous field
CTRL and X or F moves the cursor to the next field
CTRL and S moves the cursor to the previous character
CTRL and D moves the cursor to the next character
CTRL and V switches INSERT on and off
CTRL and G deletes characters at the cursor
CTRL and Y deletes an entire field

CTRL and R moves the cursor to the previous record
CTRL and C moves the cursor to the next record
CTRL and U sets (or unsets) a record for deletion
CTRL and Q exits without writing the changes to disk
CTRL and W exits and saves the changes to disk

None of the above are new: they have all been encountered in the sections on APPEND and EDIT. You may be wondering how you access the fields which could not be contained in one 80 character line; BROWSE would only have presented those fields which it could accommodate completely on a single line. Any fields to the right are not shown. Two more control keys are provided for this purpose. CTRL and B will take you to the right and present the remaining fields. It is actually moving the record to the left (under your screen window) one field at a time, but will fit in as many fields from the right as it can. Thus, moving one large field to the left so that it leaves the screen, could release screen space for 5 or 6 smaller fields which had not appeared before. CTRL and Z will do the same in reverse, i.e. move the record to the right under the screen window.

Apart from the new features of having more than one record appearing on the screen, and being able to pan the screen left and right, BROWSE follows the same rules as EDIT in that you have to use CTRL and W to save your changes.

Version 2.4 has enhanced the BROWSE command by allowing

you to specify a field list so that only selected fields are presented on the screen.

Changing the database

It would be unusual for anyone to use a database for long without finding a need to change the size of a field or add new fields. This is where a database program like dBase II really comes into its own. Unlike ordinary files, where changes create a lot of extra work, a database may be changed quite easily. To do so, you copy its structure to a new file, change the layout of the new file until it reflects your latest requirements, and then simply APPEND the data from the original file. Afterwards you may tidy up the filenames with the RENAME command.

Let us look at the procedure in more detail:

- use books
- copy structure to booksnew

The COPY command has already been described earlier in this chapter. Here it operates similarly, but instead of copying the whole database, it copies only the structure of the database. The result is an empty database which is an exact duplicate of the original. What we now want to do is to MODIFY the STRUCTURE of the empty file:

- use booksnew
- modify structure
    MODIFY ERASES ALL DATA RECORDS.....PROCEED? (Y/N)

Note the caution, but since we are dealing with an empty file we may safely reply 'Y'. A new screen appears, similar to the EDIT screen, which contains the structure details, i.e. fieldname, type, length, and the number of decimal positions. The normal editing rules apply in moving the cursor; you simply move the cursor to the item you want to change and overwrite it with your new requirement. For example:

    COST   N   005   002

becomes

    COST   N   007   002

If you want to insert a new field in the midst of others, use CTRL and N to create an empty line, and then enter the fieldname, type, length, etc., in the blank line, using the existing fields as a guide to positioning. Use CTRL and Y to delete an existing field and leave an empty line, or CTRL and T to delete an existing field completely, i.e. move subsequent ones up into its place. The important thing to remember is to use CTRL and W to save the new structure. (If you decide not to change anything and do not want to save your new changes, use CTRL and Q.) When the dot prompt appears, issue the command DISPLAY STRUCTURE and you will see your new structure. It is as well always to carry out this check after you have modified the structure of a file.

The next step consists of retrieving your data from the original file:

    .append from books

APPEND FROM

APPEND FROM will read records from the FROM database and write them to the database in USE, but only in respect of fields which have the same fieldnames in both databases. Fields which do not exist on the new database will be ignored, while new fields will be left untouched. If you have inadvertently changed the name of a field, you will find that you have not succeeded in copying that field. If the fieldnames are the same but the fields are of differing sizes, the FROM field will be expanded or truncated as necessary to fit it into the new field. Any records which had been marked for deletion will not be copied.

Following the APPEND, you will want to attend to entering data for any new fields which you have added. Any of the editing commands, i.e. EDIT, REPLACE, CHANGE or BROWSE may be used.

It is good practice to inspect your new database before you leave it to check that all is well. Any of the following commands may be used:

    LIST
    COUNT
    SUM
    DISPLAY STRUCTURE

Finally, you may tidy up the files by securing your old BOOKS file to a back-up diskette, deleting it from your working diskette, and changing the name of BOOKSNEW to BOOKS:

    . use books
    . copy to b:booksold
    . use
    . delete file books
    . rename booksnew to books

The USE command on its own closes the file. You have to do this because dBase II will not let you delete a file which is in USE. Remember also to attend to your indexes if any of your changes have affected these.

Chapter Six
dBase II in Business

A business application

To illustrate the use of several related databases, our example is going to move from its domestic environment into that of a retail organisation. We are still keeping a record of books, i.e. stock, but they are now spread over four shops instead of four bookcases. Without going into detail at this stage, we will assume that our BOOKS records contain more items of information than they did in our earlier illustration, and that we are maintaining other files, including ones which hold details of suppliers and of credit customers.

When a book is sold, the shop assistant will jot down which book it is and its price. Armed with that information, we could EDIT our way around our various databases to update the information. However, as you can imagine, it would be a tedious task. Instead, we will have the details of each day's sales put on to a temporary database and then use the latter to update our other databases automatically.

Our new application will also serve to demonstrate how to link databases for enquiry purposes. It will enable us to see, for example, how to look up details of a book following a customer enquiry and, if the book is out of stock, how to obtain and display details of the supplier's name, address and telephone number.

Updating one database from another

We are going to maintain a temporary database for each day's sales. Each temporary database will be kept until we have used it to update all our other databases. Since there could be more than one temporary database in existence at any one time, we will allocate filenames which reflect their contents, e.g. SALE1212 for the sales of December 12th.

To avoid using the CREATE function each time, we will generate each temporary database from the previous one with the COPY STRUCTURE command. It will look like this:

```
. use sale1212
. display structure
STRUCTURE FOR FILE:   SALE1212.DBF
NUMBER OF RECORDS:    00000
DATE OF LAST UPDATE:  00/00/00
PRIMARY USE DATABASE
FLD        NAME       TYPE  WIDTH    DEC
001        TITLE       C     040
002        AUTHOR      C     025
003        PRICE       N     007     002
004        CUSTCODE    C     005
005        NOBOOKS     N     002
006        SHOP        C     001
007        DATE        C     006
** TOTAL **                  00087
```

The Shop and Date fields have been placed last so that the SET CARRY ON command may be used to repeat them for each record without our having to move the cursor past them each time. When you have entered as much as you need on a screen, simply use CTRL and C to flick over the screen.

The SALE1212 file will be used to update our stock records and our credit customer records. There are other files such as suppliers' records which we could update, but let us keep it simple for now. Before entering the sales details it will be necessary to consult the Customer database to look up the customer codes which have to be entered on all sales to credit customers. If the shop assistant had sold a book to Mr M. H. James, we could obtain the latter's code as follows:

```
. use customer index custname
. find James
. display next 6 surname,initials,custcode off
James              A.A        JA001
James              C.         JA005
James              M.H.       JA003
James              P.         JA002
James              S.T.       JA004
Jason              D.F.       JA007
```

When the code for each credit customer on the sales sheets has been looked up and transcribed to the sheets, we can load the day's sales file. Use the APPEND command and let the SET CARRY ON command do as much of the work for you as possible. When entering the date, you will make things easy for yourself later on if you use the YYMMDD format, i.e. year, month, day, instead of the usual method of entering a date.

Once the job has been completed, we will list the file to provide a quick visual check on its accuracy. If you spot any errors, use one of the editing commands to correct it.

We maintain two customer files: one with details of books sold by customer, and another which holds each customer's name, address, telephone number plus some summary information that we keep for marketing purposes. It is the latter that we are about to update. It contains details of books purchased from us, their total sales value, and the date of the most recent purchase.

What we want to do is to run our SALE1212 file against this Customer file and match on the Custcode field. When a match is found we want to add the number of books and their price from the sales record to the customer record, and replace the date field on the customer record with that from the sales record. This is how:

- use customer index custcode
- update on custcode from sale1212 add nosold,price; replace date

There are two points of notice:

(1) The fieldnames on both databases have to be the same for any fields which are used in the UPDATE command. Version 2.4 will let you use different fieldnames in the REPLACE clause.

(2) Both databases must be in the same sequence, i.e. that of the key specified by the ON clause (Custcode in our example). This is the key on which the two databases will be matched. The main database, i.e. that in USE, may be indexed or sorted on the key. The FROM database must be sorted on the key. Version 2.4 will let you have an unsorted FROM database if you specify RANDOM in the UPDATE command and provided the main database is indexed on the key rather than sorted on it. It gets round the unsorted sequence of the FROM file by carrying out an internal FIND on the main database and you will remember, of course, that FIND operates on an index.

(3) It does not matter if there is more than one record on the FROM

database which matches a single record on the main database; dBase II will simply repeat the update. Take care, however, that your REPLACE actions will work out the way you expect because, in such a situation, it will be the last record encountered for a given match that will update the field to be replaced. In our example, it does not matter if there are several sales records for the same customer because the REPLACE field, i.e. the date, will be the same on each record.

Let us now turn to our stock file, i.e. BOOKS, and update that to reflect for each title the number of books sold to date and their total sales value:

```
. use books index titles
. update on title from sale1212 add nosold,price
```

Incidentally, the titles index need not contain each title in full. UPDATE will work with a substring of a field provided it starts at the beginning of the field. In our example, the titles have been indexed as follows:

```
. use books
. index on $(title,1,20) to titles
```

To round off this section on the UPDATE command, let us look at a complete example using specimen sales and stock files:

```
. use sale1212
. list title,nosold,price
00001  As You Like It                        2    3.98
00002  Dombey and Son                        2    4.76
00003  Far from the Madding Crowd            1    2.99

. use books index titles
. list title,nosold,price
00001  As You Like It                        1    1.50
00016  Bleak House                           1    4.00
00014  Canterbury Tales                      0    0.00
00017  Crime and Punishment                  0    0.00
00008  Devon and Cornwall                    1    2.50
00003  Dombey and Son                        0    0.00
00006  Far from the Madding Crowd            3    6.00
00012  Formation of England,The              0    0.00
00013  Henry V                               4    8.00
00010  Indian Dishes                         1    4.00
00007  Islands of Greece,The                 0    0.00
00011  Kings and Queens of England           5   12.50
00009  Microwave Cookery                     0    0.00
00002  Pride and Prejudice                   3    9.00
00004  Treasure Island                       1    4.00
00005  Turn of the Screw                     0    0.00
```

```
00015  War and Peace                          0    0.00
. update on title from sale1212 add nosold,price
. list title,nosold,price
00001  As You Like It                         3    5.48
00016  Bleak House                            1    4.00
00014  Canterbury Tales                       0    0.00
00017  Crime and Punishment                   0    0.00
00008  Devon and Cornwall                     1    2.50
00003  Dombey and Son                         2    4.76
00006  Far from the Madding Crowd             4    8.99
00012  Formation of England,The               0    0.00
00013  Henry V                                4    8.00
00010  Indian Dishes                          1    4.00
00007  Islands of Greece,The                  0    0.00
00011  Kings and Queens of England            5   12.50
00009  Microwave Cookery                      0    0.00
00002  Pride and Prejudice                    3    9.00
00004  Treasure Island                        1    4.00
00005  Turn of the Screw                      0    0.00
00015  War and Peace                          0    0.00
```

Using two databases

One of the advantages of our computer system is that we maintain a readily accessible record of all our stock so that any customer enquiry can be satisfied very quickly. If, say, we are asked if we have a copy of Tom Sawyer, we could do the following:

```
. use books index titles
. find Tom Sawyer
. display shops,nobought,nosold,supcode,title off
a,c         6    4 BW Tom Sawyer
```

That would show us that we had purchased 6 copies, sold 4 to date, and that shops a and c still had copies. If, however, we discovered that we had sold all our copies, we would want to know which supplier to ring to order extra copies and to find out when they could be delivered. With limited suppliers, a supplier code would probably be all we need, but let us assume that we have a large number of suppliers and that we need to look up their details.

We could, of course, switch to the supplier file and use the supplier code to look up the required details but we would then be closing and opening files with each successive USE. A faster method of switching between two databases is to declare one as primary and the other as secondary, open both at the same time (i.e. USE both) and then select whichever you need for a given item of information. Switching from one to the other does not disturb the

58 Working With dBase II

positioning of the current record in either. The following shows how it is done:

```
. use books index titles
. select secondary
. use supplier index suppind
. select primary
```

SELECT SECONDARY

SELECT PRIMARY

By means of the SELECT SECONDARY command we have switched to our supplier file, opened it with the USE command, and switched back with the SELECT PRIMARY command. We will now do some work with the two files. Remember that at the start of the following sequence of commands we are back in PRIMARY, i.e. the BOOKS database:

```
. find Tom Sawyer
. display supcode,title off
BW  Tom Sawyer
. select secondary
. find BW
. display name,phone off
Book Wholesalers           204-7149
```

The supplier file is indexed on the supplier code so that we are able to access the supplier with the FIND command. We then display his name and telephone number.

A useful feature of primary and secondary files is that one may use information from one while in the other. If the fieldnames are identical, you get around it by prefixing the fieldname with a 'p.' or 's.' to indicate primary and secondary respectively. The following is an example of using fields from both databases:

```
. use supplier index suppind
. select secondary
. use books index supplier
. select primary
. find BW
. select secondary
. find BW
. display next 4 for supcode="BW" name,cost,title off    off
Book Wholesalers        0.99 As You Like It
Book Wholesalers        2.50 Canterbury Tales
Book Wholesalers        2.50 Dombey and Son
Book Wholesalers        3.99 Treasure Island
```

The DISPLAY command has listed information from both databases while in the secondary database – in this case, our

BOOKS file. More than two databases may be referenced in this way, but only two may be in USE at any one time.

The example above has left us in the secondary database. We should therefore finish by returning to the primary database with a further SELECT PRIMARY (or SELE PRIM) command. In our example we have not performed any updating on the secondary database. Had we done so, we should also close the secondary database with a USE command before returning to the primary database to ensure that all changes and additions have been written to the file. We would add the following to the example:

```
. use
. select primary
. use
```

The final USE would close the primary database. Another method of closing files is to use the CLEAR command. This command does not require you to select one or other database: it will close both databases automatically. It will also clear all temporary fields, i.e. memory variables.

Copying and joining databases

So far, we have discussed the COPY command in two forms: copying an entire database as it stands, and copying the structure of a database. Accompanying the latter was the APPEND FROM command. We are now going to see what else we can do with these commands.

Let us begin with a simple extension of the COPY command. Say that we had wanted to change the database not by adding fields or changing the sizes of existing fields, but by dropping a field. We could, of course, use the MODIFY STRUCTURE command to delete the field from a copy of the structure and then use APPEND FROM to bring in the data for the remaining fields. Or we could use an extra facility of the COPY command which allows us to specify which fields we want to copy. We would thus include all fieldnames except the unwanted ones. The keyword FIELD must precede the fieldnames. The example below shows the structure of the supplier file and the results of the COPY command:

```
. use supplier
. display structure
STRUCTURE FOR FILE:    SUPPLIER.DBF
```

```
NUMBER OF RECORDS:     00173
DATE OF LAST UPDATE:   09/09/84
PRIMARY USE DATABASE
FLD         NAME           TYPE   WIDTH      DEC
001         CODE            C     002
002         NAME            C     035
003         ADDR1           C     035
004         ADDR2           C     035
005         ADDR3           C     035
006         ADDR4           C     035
007         PHONE           C     010
** TOTAL **                       00188

. copy to suppx fields code,name,phone

. use suppx
. display structure
STRUCTURE FOR FILE:    SUPPX.DBF
NUMBER OF RECORDS:     00173
DATE OF LAST UPDATE:   09/09/84
PRIMARY USE DATABASE
FLD         NAME           TYPE   WIDTH      DEC
001         CODE            C     002
002         NAME            C     035
003         PHONE           C     010
** TOTAL **                       00048

. disp next 4
00001   BW Book Wholesalers              204-7149
00002   CA Caxton Book Sales             204-8686
00003   MA Maxi Book Suppliers           440-5141
00004   ND National Book Distributers    556-7808
```

The COPY command also contains a scope clause – for example, NEXT 20 – and the FOR or WHILE conditional clauses. You could thus copy only those records which meet a specified condition. For example:

```
. use books
. display next 9 author,class
00001   Shakespeare          Drama
00002   Austen,Jane          Novel
00003   Dickens              Novel
00004   Stevenson,R L        Novel
00005   James,Henry          Novel
00006   Hardy,Thomas         Novel
00007   Jones,T B            Travel
00008   Hall,F J             Travel
00009   Jones,Belinda        Cooking

. copy to books2 fields author,nosold,supcode for class="Novel"
```

```
. use books2
. display next 5
00001   Austen,Jane                      3 MA
00002   Dickens                          2 BW
00003   Stevenson,R L                    1 BW
00004   James,Henry                      0 CA
00005   Hardy,Thomas                     4 CA
```

The APPEND FROM command could similarly be made to accept only those records which meet the FOR or WHILE conditions:

```
. use books
. copy structure to novels
. use novels
. append from books for class="Novel"
. go top
. disp next 5 author,class
00001   Austen,Jane                      Novel
00002   Dickens                          Novel
00003   Stevenson,R L                    Novel
00004   James,Henry                      Novel
00005   Hardy,Thomas                     Novel
```

What if you wanted to combine the contents of two dissimilar databases? Let us say that you wanted to create a new file containing data from both the BOOKS and the SUPPLIER files. First, you would have to define each database:

```
. use books
. select secondary
. use supplier
. select primary
```

Next, you issue the JOIN command:

JOIN

```
. join to booksupp for supcode=code fields title,author,code,phone
```

Let us first look at the result and then the command will be explained.

```
. use booksupp
. disp next 7 code,phone,author,trim(title)
00001   BW 204-7149   Shakespeare      As You Like It
00002   MA 440-5141   Austen,Jane      Pride and Prejudice
00003   BW 204-7149   Dickens          Dombey and Son
00004   BW 204-7149   Stevenson,R L    Treasure Island
00005   CA 204-8686   James,Henry      Turn of the Screw
00006   CA 204-8686   Hardy,Thomas     Far from the Madding Crowd
00007   CA 204-8686   Jones,T B        Islands of Greece,The
```

When we issued the JOIN command, dBase II started with the first record on the primary database and read through the whole of the secondary database, comparing the primary field Supcode with the secondary field Code. When it found a match, it wrote the requested field from both records to the specified database, in this case BOOKSUPP. The structure of the latter was determined by the fields specified in the JOIN command. When dBase II had read through to the end of the secondary file, it moved on to the second record on the primary file and read through the secondary file again, looking for a match on the two fields. This sequence was repeated until every record on the primary file had been read, i.e. the secondary file was read as many times as there are records on the primary file.

When specifying fieldnames which are the same on both files, remember to provide the 'p.' or 's.' prefix which tells dBase II whether the field is on the primary or the secondary database. The condition specified in the JOIN command need not be restricted to the matching fields. You could extend it to include other criteria. For example:

```
. join to booksupp for supcode=code .and. class="Novel";
                         fields author,code,phone
. use booksupp
. display next 8
00001   Austen,Jane           MA 440-5141
00002   Dickens               BW 204-7149
00003   Stevenson,R L         BW 204-7149
00004   James,Henry           CA 204-8686
00005   Hardy,Thomas          CA 204-8686
00006   Tolstoy               MA 440-5141
00007   Dickens               BW 204-7149
00008   Dostoievsky           CA 204-8686
```

The potential number of records that could be created by the JOIN command is equal to the total number of records on the primary database multiplied by the total number of records on the secondary database. Also, if you do not specify a list of fields, the structure of the specified database will contain all the fields from the primary database plus all the fields from the secondary database, even if the same fieldname was on both databases.

Review

Although Part 1 provided you with the major techniques for using dBase II, Part 2 has shown you how to be more sophisticated in your use of the database. That is not to say that you could not have continued to manage quite well without the use of any of the commands described in Part 2. That part of Chapter 5 which deals with changing the database is probably the only exception, but it very much follows the pattern of Part 1 in being a simple and direct procedure.

We now move on to more complex methods in Part 3. These will involve you in writing procedural sequences of commands. The actual commands remain simple, but the way in which they are put together will require a greater involvement on your part.

Part 3
Programming with dBase II

Chapter Seven
Writing dBase II Programs

What is a dBase II program?

A program is a series of commands which you have stored on a diskette. Most of the dBase II commands you have already encountered may be stored in this way. Admittedly, the earlier part of this book concentrated on commands which could be used either singly or with little dependence on other commands, and you may be wondering what need there is for storing them on a diskette when they could perfectly well be entered as you need them. The answer lies partly in repetition. As soon as you have a method which is used repetitively, it becomes easier simply to tap in the filename of the stored dBase II commands (known as a command file) as follows:

.do findbook

In the above example, the file FINDBOOK contains the dBase II commands, and the DO command retrieves them from the diskette and executes them.

Other reasons for using a command file are that by writing programs you are able to provide facilities for the non-technical user, and you can create applications which are far more sophisticated than those which would otherwise be possible.

The next question to be answered is: How does one get the commands into a diskette file? There is nothing special about the file of commands except that each command is expected on a new line. You may, therefore, use any means open to you of storing data on a diskette, including the use of a word processing package. dBase II has its own file editor which may be used to create a file or subsequently change it. This editor is summoned by issuing the MODIFY COMMAND command (MODI COMM for short) followed by the filename of the command file. You will be presented with a blank screen if the file does not exist, otherwise the stored

68 *Working With dBase II*

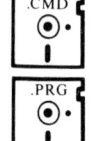

dBase II commands will be retrieved from the command file and shown on the screen. All the normal editing rules apply, and you may enter or change as necessary, finishing with CTRL and W to save the file. Command files are identified by a suffix of .CMD on CP/M systems and .PRG on 16-bit systems such as PC-DOS. The FINDBOOK command file will thus appear as follows on the diskette:

FINDBOOK.CMD or FINDBOOK.PRG

However, neither **MODIFY COMMAND** nor the DO command requires you to specify the suffix. They will both add the suffix automatically. The previous version of the FINDBOOK command file, if there had been one, would have been renamed as FINDBOOK.BAK.

Having discussed how to create a command file, and how to use one, let us look more closely at the contents of such a file.

How to start

We have already seen that the DISPLAY, LIST and REPORT commands enable us to produce information reports on the data we have stored in the database. Yet, each of these left something to be desired. DISPLAY and LIST could not provide sub-totals, page control, etc., and REPORT would only operate in a fixed tabular format. Suppose you wanted to produce a formatted page such as an invoice, or wanted to list all items for a given classification but show the classification only at the top of the page. It is to meet these and many other needs that one turns to the dBase II programming facilities.

For reporting purposes, a program typically reads through the database making decisions on the way and producing print lines as it goes along. There are many situations where your program will not need to read through the database, i.e. it will consult an index and extract only the requisite records, but let us accept for now that we want to access every record in the database in much the same way as the LIST, LOCATE, SUM, REPORT, etc., commands do. In these commands, dBase II takes care of moving from one record to another and applying to each one the necessary criteria requested as part of the command.

When you write a program, however, you have to spell it all out yourself. For example, to move from one record to another you have to issue the SKIP command. You will not, however, want to issue as many SKIP commands as there are records in the database. You therefore need a command which will repeat a set of commands until all records have been examined. This is the DO WHILE command. In this case, we want to DO WHILE it is not the end of the file, i.e. carry on until the end of the file is reached. At that point the last record will have been examined, and we will thus have completed our task of accessing every record in the database. The command looks like this:

```
do while .not.eof
```

Notice the absence of the dot prompt: there is no need for a prompt in a command file. You may prefer to use capitals, or even a mixture of upper- and lower-case: dBase II will accept both. We will continue to use lower-case.

DO WHILE is an incomplete command: it needs an ENDDO to tell it which commands it should DO, i.e. any commands following the DO WHILE command up to before the ENDDO command. Let us look at a simple command file which will perform exactly the same function as DISPLAY TITLE FOR AUTHOR="Dickens":

```
* Title Display
set talk off
use books
do while .not.eof
  if author = "Dickens"
    display title
  endif
  skip
enddo
```

In the example above, the DO WHILE command will see to the repetition of the subsequent commands until the end of the file is reached. The SKIP command performs the task of actually moving on to the next record. It performs an essential function, since otherwise you would repeat the command sequence endlessly on record 00001 without moving any further towards the end of the file.

You will also notice that we are having to perform for ourselves a test which is carried out automatically by the FOR clause of the DISPLAY command. The IF command is another paired command: it needs ENDIF to tell it where to stop paying attention to the conditions which apply to the selection. In the example above, nothing will happen if the condition is not met, i.e. if the author is not Dickens. Such records will simply be by-passed. Records which do meet the condition will have the title field displayed. For example:

```
00001    Bleak House
00002    Dombey and Son
```

The SET TALK OFF command prevents dBase II from displaying record numbers as it progresses through the file. Without the SET TALK OFF, the number of each record on the file would be displayed as a result of the SKIP command. For example:

```
00001    Bleak House
RECORD: 00002
00002    Dombey and Son
RECORD: 00003
RECORD: 00004
RECORD: 00005
```

Another dBase II command, the *, may be used to provide comments such as ones which will afterwards remind you of the purpose of the command file. An alternative to the * command is the NOTE command which has exactly the same function. These may be placed anywhere in a command file. dBase II will ignore them when it is executing the command file.

In summary, we have managed to create a series of commands which have allowed us to examine every record in the database, applied a selection condition, and displayed a field from every record which met that selection.

It is not a lot when you consider that the DISPLAY command could equal all that with considerably less effort. It is, however, the foundation of a very powerful set of facilities, all of which rely on your being able to have complete control over the way in which dBase II uses the information in the database.

Programming a report

Some of the major elements of producing a report have already been discussed in the preceding section but there are a small number of other important commands to be covered.

(1) The first is a combination which works hand-in-hand to indicate the fields to be shown on a report as well as specifying where on the report they are to appear.

@ provides the line number and position on the line, and SAY indicates the information which is to be printed at that position. For example:

    @ 1,30 say "LIST OF BOOKS BY SUPPLIER"

The first line on a page (or the screen for that matter) is always line 0. The first position, i.e. the left-most, is position 0. On a screen, the final position is 79, but on a printer it extends to the widest point the printer is able to produce, to a maximum of 254. When displaying details on the screen, try to avoid using line 0 since dBase II uses that line to display messages to the user.

(2) There is another command, the ? command, which may be used to position data on a screen or print line. With this command, you show the items exactly as you want to see them by positioning them to the right of blank spaces. For example:

    ? "   LIST OF BOOKS BY SUPPLIER"

The quote marks tell dBase II to count each space enclosed within them as a character, albeit a blank one. The heading will thus be positioned as you see it. The ? command has already been encountered as a means of displaying the contents of a temporary field or memory variable. Here it is displaying the data contained between the quote marks.

The ? command on its own may be used to space down a screen or printed report. Each ? will space one line. Used twice, i.e. ??, as a display command it will produce the data on the same line as the previous command. In other words, it will not space down. For example:

    ? "SHOP A"   LIST OF BOOKS BY SUPPLIER"
    ?? "

will produce

    SHOP A   LIST OF BOOKS BY SUPPLIER

(3) Temporary fields are quite important in a dBase II program in that you will need temporary fields to keep track of such things as page numbers or lines on a page. These temporary fields or memory variables are used quite easily: you simply allocate a name and use the name in a command to establish it as a field. For example:

    store 1 to pageno

A character memory variable will be as long as the character field which has been stored to it. Logical memory variables, e.g. ones containing a logical value such as T for True or F for False, are, always one character in length. A numeric memory variable occupies 6 characters or bytes of memory and can store a maximum of 10 digits. The important thing to bear in mind here is that a numeric memory variable used in an @ SAY command will occupy 10 positions on your report or on the screen, even when it contains no more than a single digit. This means that when you are positioning a numeric memory variable in relation to a field from a database record, say as a total of that field, you have to allow for the difference in size between the two fields. Let us look at an example where we have been accumulating the four-digit field Nosold into a memory variable called Totsold:

```
@ 5,30 say nosold
@ 6,30 say "----"
@ 7,30 say totsold
@ 8,30 say "===="
```

This is how it will appear:

```
                  25
                  ----
                          25
                  ====
```

If, however, the size difference of the two fields had been taken into account, they would have been positioned liked this:

```
@ 5,30 say nosold
@ 6,30 say "----"
@ 7,24 say totsold
@ 8,30 say "===="
```

and would appear as:

```
                  25
                  ----
                  25
                  ====
```

Another method of positioning numeric memory variables is to use the STR function which converts a numeric field to a character field:

```
@ 5,30 say nosold
@ 6,30 say "----"
@ 7,30 say str(totsold,4)
@ 8,30 say "===="
```

(4) You have also just encountered a new and essential command: STORE. To set a field, e.g. the page number, to an initial value such as "1", you use STORE. You also use STORE to increment the field. For example:

    store pageno + 1 to pageno

You may STORE a value to several fields in the same command. For example:

    store 0 to lines,pageno

(5) Finally, if you are using a printer, it will be necessary to move the paper to the start of the page (or head of form) before the perforation line is reached, or if you decide to start a new page on change of, say, supplier. This is done with the EJECT command.

Let us look at an example which is first given in full and then explained in sections. We are going to list the books from three of our suppliers. We will print the report heading on each page and throw to a new page (EJECT) on change of supplier. The file will have to be in supplier sequence otherwise we will be unable to collect together all the records for each supplier.

```
set print on
set format to print
set talk off
use books index booksup
store " " to supcodex
store 0 to pageno,lines
do while .not. eof
  if supcode="BW" .or. supcode="CA" .or. supcode="MA"
    if supcode#supcodex
      store 57 to lines
      store supcode to supcodex
    endif
    if lines > 56
      eject
      store pageno + 1 to pageno
      @ 1,1 say "Page "+str(pageno,3)
      @ 1,30 say "List of Books supplied by "+supcode
      store 3 to lines
    endif
    @ lines,1 say title
    store lines + 1 to lines
  endif
  skip
```

```
enddo
eject
set print off
set format to screen
set talk on
```

[SET PRINT] Note that the SET PRINT ON and the SET FORMAT TO PRINT commands have been used at the beginning of the command file to direct the report to the printer. The SET FORMAT TO PRINT command is necessary when you have used the @ command. It directs the @ SAY elements to the printer. If we had used only ? commands, SET PRINT ON would have been sufficient. The SET TALK OFF command is necessary to avoid printing dBase II responses such as the record number each time the SKIP command is executed. At the end of the command file the EJECT command is used to flush any remaining print lines out of the print buffer, and the screen is reinstated as the display device. The above will produce the following:

```
Page    1               List of Books supplied by BW
As You Like It
Dombey and Son
Treasure Island
Canterbury Tales

Page    2               List of Books supplied by CA
Turn of the Screw
Far from the Madding Crowd
Islands of Greece,The
Kings and Queens of England

Page    3               List of Books supplied by MA
Pride and Prejudice
Devon and Cornwall
Microwave Cookery
Indian Dishes
Formation of England,The
Henry V
```

Another point you may notice is that dBase II will not let you use a memory variable in an IF command unless you have first initialised it with a STORE command. This will tell dBase II whether it is a character or numeric field and how long it is. In the example above, the field Supcodex was initialised as a character field with a length of 2 characters.

The controlling command sequence, if extracted from the above would be:

```
do while .not. eof
   if supcode="BW" .or. supcode="CA" .or. supcode="MA"
      @ lines,1 say title
      store lines + 1 to lines
   endif
   skip
enddo
```

Let us see what would happen if we put the above, on its own, into a framework that would do no more than print the results of the command sequence:

```
set print on
set format to print
set talk off
use books index booksup
store 1 to lines
do while .not. eof
   if supcode="BW" .or. supcode="CA" .or. supcode="MA"
      @ lines,1 say title
      store lines + 1 to lines
   endif
   skip
enddo
eject
set print off
set format to screen
```

We have introduced one extra command line; we had to initialise the memory variable Lines to 1 whereas in the full example, Lines was initialised as part of printing the page heading. However, the above, as it stands and with none of the other commands, will present the required information to us. It will be without a break at the end of a page or change of supplier and will not tell us which supplier provided which books, but as a command file it will work. It will simply list the books supplied by the three selected suppliers:

```
As You Like It
Dombey and Son
Treasure Island
Canterbury Tales
Turn of the Screw
Far from the Madding Crowd
Islands of Greece,The
```

```
    Kings and Queens of England
    Pride and Prejudice
    Devon and Cornwall
    Microwave Cookery
    Indian Dishes
    Formation of England,The
    Henry V
```

The major points to notice are:

- The SKIP command which moves the command sequence on to the next record.
- The use of the temporary field Lines to advance the printing on to the next line.
- the indentation of the commands which does not affect their execution in any way, but shows clearly which group of commands belong together.

If you look back at the full example you will see that the other actions are performed within the controlling command sequence:

(1) Before printing a line, we test the line positioning and when it reaches the end of the page, we EJECT to the top of the next page, print the page heading, and reset the line positioning. You will see that the page heading combines two fields with the + operator. The latter may be used to join character fields. The STR function reduces the size of the Pageno field to three characters.

(2) Before doing the foregoing, we compare the supplier code of each selected record with the stored supplier code, i.e. that from the previous selected record. If different, we force an EJECT to a new page by moving a high value into the memory variable which controls line positioning. Note, also, that the supplier code from the new record is immediately stored, ready for testing against subsequent records.

Having started with this comparatively simple report, you may now embroider the above to show the full supplier name, print extra fields, show a count of the number of books found for each supplier, or sum the numeric fields. We will use the technique explained in Chapter 6, of obtaining information from a second database, to show the full supplier name:

```
set print on
set format to print
set talk off
```

```
use books index booksup
select secondary
use supplier index suppind
select primary
store "  " to supcodex
store 0 to pageno,lines
do while .not. eof
   if supcode="BW" .or. supcode="CA" .or. supcode="MA"
      if supcode#supcodex
         store 57 to lines
         store supcode to supcodex
         select secondary
         find &supcodex
         select primary
      endif
      if lines > 56
         eject
         store pageno + 1 to pageno
         @ 1,1 say "Page "+str(pageno,3)
         @ 1,30 say "List of Books supplied by "+name
         store 3 to lines
      endif
      @ lines,1 say title
      store lines + 1 to lines
   endif
   skip
enddo
eject
set print off
set format to screen
```

You should observe two further points here. In the section on using two databases in Chapter 6, the FIND command operated on actual data, i.e. we supplied the title of a book as part of the command itself. Here we are asking the FIND command to go and look at the contents of a memory variable and to search on that. To differentiate between data and the name of a memory variable, we prefix the latter with the macro substitute character (&). Secondly, we are now displaying the full name of the supplier in the page heading by taking it from the secondary database.

Let us next turn to displaying some extra fields and providing sub-totals of these. For example, to add the number of copies bought and sold, you could follow the @ SAY command line which displays the title with two more:

78 Working With dBase II

```
@ lines,45 say nobought
@ lines,55 say nosold
```

To sum each of these fields, you would employ two memory variables and add the following lines:

```
store totbought + nobought to totbought
store totsold + nosold to totsold
```

You could not use the SUM command itself, because it does more than add fields into a total: it also reads through the database to do so. Since you are yourself reading through the database, you do not want the current record reset by any of the commands you are using. Remember, also, that both Totbought and Totsold have to be initialised before using them. If the above had read

```
store nobought to totbought
store nosold to totsold
```

they would have been initialised there and then, but the use of the + operator demands that they are initialised earlier.

The memory variables Totbought and Totsold could be printed before we EJECT the page on change of author, i.e. immediately following the test for change of supplier:

```
if supcode#supcodex
   store lines + 1 to lines
   @ lines,1   say "Total"
   @ lines,39 say totbought
   @ lines,49 say totsold
   store 57 to lines
endif
```

There are two further problems:

(1) The above will print Totbought and Totsold before we print the first page heading, because on the very first record the supplier code will be different to the content of the temporary field Supcodex (which was initialised by storing two spaces to it). We will thus need to add a 'first-time-thru' test. For example:

```
if supcode#supcodex
  if supcodex#"  "
     store lines + 1 to lines
     @ lines,1   say "Total"
     @ lines,39 say totbought
     @ lines,49 say totsold
  endif
```

```
    store 57 to lines
endif
```

(2) The second problem stems from the fact that we are printing the totals for the previous supplier on change of supplier. What will happen, however, at the end of the file when we also reach the end of a supplier, but not on a change of supplier? The program will simply stop repeating the commands contained between the DO WHILE and ENDDO commands and go on to commands following the ENDDO. It would be logical then to place the printing of the final supplier's totals after the ENDDO. For example:

```
enddo
store lines + 1 to lines
@ lines,1  say "Total"
@ lines,39 say totbought
@ lines,49 say totsold
eject
set print off
set format to screen
```

The whole sequence looks like this:

```
set print on
set format to print
set talk off
use books index booksup
select secondary
use supplier index suppind
select primary
store "  " to supcodex
store 0 to pageno,lines,totbought,totsold
do while .not. eof
  if supcode="BW" .or. supcode="CA" .or. supcode="MA"
    if supcode#supcodex
      if supcodex#"  "
        store lines + 1 to lines
        @ lines,1 say "Total"
        @ lines,39 say totbought
        @ lines,49 say totsold
        store 0 to totbought,totsold
      endif
      store 57 to lines
      store supcode to supcodex
      select secondary
      find &supcodex
      select primary
```

```
endif
if lines > 56
  eject
  store pageno + 1 to pageno
  @ 1,1 say "Page "+str(pageno,3)
  @ 1,30 say "List of Books supplied by "+name
  @ 3,45 say "No Bought"
  @ 3,55 say "No Sold"
  store 5 to lines
endif
@ lines,1 say title
@ lines,45 say nobought
@ lines,55 say nosold
store totbought + nobought to totbought
store totsold + nosold to totsold
store lines + 1 to lines
  endif
  skip
enddo
store lines + 1 to lines
@ lines,1 say "Total"
@ lines,39 say totbought
@ lines,49 say totsold
eject
set print off
set format to screen
return
```

We have suffixed the complete command sequence with the RETURN command. The latter signals the end of the command file and allows dBase II to close the command file. It is good practice to finish off a command file in this way since there is a limit of 16 on the number of files (including the database itself) which the program will let you have open at a time. It may seem an unlikely event at the moment, but once you have several command files and a menu from which to call them up, you will soon run into the 'TOO MANY FILES ARE OPEN' message. Using RETURN will avoid that.

Let us look at the report produced by the complete command file:

```
Page   1              List of Books supplied by Book Wholesalers

                                       No Bought  No Sold

As You Like It                             4         3
Dombey and Son                             2         2
Treasure Island                            1         1
Canterbury Tales                           1         0

Total                                      8         6
```

Page 2   List of Books supplied by Caxton Book Sales

                                    No Bought No Sold

Turn of the Screw   2   0
Far from the Madding Crowd   6   4
Islands of Greece,The   1   1
Kings and Queens of England   6   5

Total   15   10

Page 3   List of Books supplied by Maxi Book Suppliers

                                    No Bought No Sold

Pride and Prejudice   4   3
Devon and Cornwall   1   1
Microwave Cookery   1   0
Indian Dishes   2   1
Formation of England,The   1   0
Henry V   6   4

Total   15   9

Writing an enquiry program

Let us turn from the production of reports, to the production of screens for enquiry purposes. We would like to allow a user to walk up to the screen, enter his or her request for information (without having to use any dBase II language), and see the results appear on the screen.

We will shortly discuss menus which provide a list of options covering several different types of enquiry, but let us concentrate for now on a single enquiry which will repeat the facility offered in the section on using two databases in Chapter 6 – that of being able to find out whether we have a requested title in stock at any of our four shops. This time, however, it has been converted for the use of non-technical staff.

First of all, we need to provide a screen which may be called up by the person making the enquiry. The screen should contain text describing its purpose, prompts (e.g. 'Enter Title') and empty fields where the user will enter his data. For example:

TITLE ENQUIRY

Enter Title   :   :

82 Working With dBase II

We will need three commands:

(1) STORE to set up the memory variable which is to receive the data entered by the user.

[@ GET]

(2) @ SAY GET to display the prompt and demarcate an area on the screen for data entry. The GET clause is simply an addition to the @ command.

[READ]

(3) READ to move the entered information from the screen to the memory variable.

It is worth being clear on one point: GET does no more than display a field which may be edited to the screen. The READ command does the work of taking the data from the screen and moving it back into the field.

The command file which produces the Title Enquiry screen is as follows:

```
@ 1,30   say "TITLE ENQUIRY"
store "                                         " to titlex
@ 5,0    say "Enter Title   " get titlex
read
```

Now that the READ command has placed the requested title in the Titlex field, we are back in familiar territory. We use the FIND command to get the required record on the database and we then display its details. The command file, which we are going to call BOOKENQ, looks like this:

```
use books index titles
@ 1,30   say "TITLE ENQUIRY"
store "                                         " to titlex
@ 5,0    say "Enter Title   " get titlex
read
find &titlex
store nobought - nosold to stock
@ 9,0    say "Title              "+title
@ 11,0   say "Author             "+author
@ 13,0   say "Classification     "+class
@ 15,0   say "Supplier Code      "+supcode
@ 17,0   say "No. Copies in Stock "
@ 17,22  say stock
@ 19,0   say "Shops              "+shops
```

Note the use of the STORE command to do the subtraction which provides us with a net stock figure. Note also that you cannot join a numeric field like Stock to a character field like "No. Copies in Stock" with the '+' operator. The latter will only concatenate (i.e. join) character fields. In the command file we simply used an extra

Writing dBase II Programs 83

@ SAY to display the contents of the Stock field on the same line as the character field.

As an example of the command file in action, the following will be displayed on receiving an enquiry for *War and Peace*:

Title	War and Peace
Author	Tolstoy
Classification	Novel
Supplier Code	BW
No. Copies in Stock	2
Shops	a,d

We could go on to write the commands which would obtain the supplier details in the event of nil stock, but let us instead spend some more time on what we have done so far. You will remember that a command file is executed by the DO statement, which specifies the name of the command file. For example:

```
do bookenq
```

The command file we have created so far will only work for a single enquiry, and will then return you to the dBase II dot prompt. We could call it up each time we needed to make an enquiry by issuing a DO command, but we would be better off leaving the enquiry facility on the screen until we need a different type of enquiry or want to use the computer for something else. We will thus need the DO WHILE and ENDDO commands in our command file. This time, however, we cannot use the EOF test in the DO WHILE command because we are not reading through a file. What we will do is to set up a condition and let the DO WHILE test it. For example:

```
store "T" to continue
do while continue = "T"
```

We will also explain to the user that when he wants to stop using the enquiry he should press the return key without supplying a title. We will then provide a test in the command file which will check for spaces in the title (i.e. a blank title) and, if found, change the "T" in Continue to an "F". DO WHILE will then find an unequal comparison and the program will resume at the command following ENDDO:

```
use books index titles
store "T" to continue
do while continue="T"
  @ 1,30  say "TITLE ENQUIRY"
  store "                              " to titlex
  @ 5,0  say "Enter Title  " get titlex
  read
  if titlex=" "
    store "F" to continue
  else
    find &titlex
    store nobought - nosold to stock
    @ 9,0   say "Title              "+title
    @ 11,0  say "Author             "+author
    @ 13,0  say "Classification     "+class
    @ 15,0  say "Supplier Code      "+supcode
    @ 17,0  say "No. Copies in Stock "
    @ 17,22 say stock
    @ 19,0  say "Shops              "+shops
  endif
enddo
```

In the above example, we stored the characters "T" and "F" to a memory variable. As it happens, T and F may also be used as logical expressions to represent true or false. You may therefore use them without the quote marks. Moreover, a memory variable which contains a logical expression may be tested without using the equals sign. For example:

```
store T to continue
do while continue
```

The DO WHILE test is asking, in effect, whether Continue is true or not. It is true if it contains a T, not true if it does not. If you had stored F to Continue, you could have tested it with the .NOT. operator. For example:

```
do while .not. continue
```

Variations on the above are:

```
"T", "t", "Y", or "y" for true

"F", "f", "N", or "n" for false
```

Yet another approach to the DO WHILE command is to provide a permanent DO. For example:

```
do while T
```

Writing dBase II Programs

This DO will remain in force until the RETURN command is issued. In our example, we end the DO WHILE condition by replacing

```
if titlex=" "
    store "F" to continue
else
```

with

```
if titlex=" "
    return
else
```

There is another aspect of the command file which needs attention. Suppose that the FIND command does not find the requested author? We ought to test for an unsuccessful FIND and report back to the user.

The method for checking a successful FIND relies on the record number of the "found" record. Following a successful FIND, the record number will be stored in the dBase II field which contains the current record number. If the FIND was unsuccessful, the current record number would be set to zero. We are thus in a position to examine this field to determine whether we "found" the record or not. The current record number field is examined by the function #. For example:

```
if # = 0
    @ 11,1 say titlex+" Not Found"
endif
```

Let us look at the complete command file with a small number of additions:

```
use books index titles
erase
do while T
  @ 1,30  say "TITLE ENQUIRY"
  store "                              " to titlex
  @ 5,0   say "Enter Title    " get titlex
  read
  if titlex=" "
    erase
    return
  else
    find &titlex
    if #=0
      @ 11,1 say titlex+" Not Found"
    else
      store nobought - nosold to stock
      @ 9,0   say "Title                "+title
```

```
    @ 11,0    say "Author                    "+author
    @ 13,0    say "Classification            "+class
    @ 15,0    say "Supplier Code             "+supcode
    @ 17,0    say "No. Copies in Stock       "
    @ 17,22   say stock
    @ 19,0    say "Shops                     "+shops
  endif
  @ 23,0   say "Press any key to continue"
  wait
  erase
endif
enddo
```

The above has brought together the following:

(1) The original example of providing a user with a means of entering a request, finding the requested record, and then displaying the results.

(2) The DO WHILE T method of keeping the program active for as long as we need it, together with an escape route which uses the RETURN command to leave the program.

(3) The refinement of telling the user whether we found his request or not.

The command file also contains minor additions. These are all related to control of the screen. A screen does not automatically erase all currently displayed data simply because you have decided to display a new set of details. You have to clear away the old details yourself by using the ERASE command which has the simple job of wiping the whole screen clear. It is thus very useful to start a command file with the ERASE command.

You may also want to erase, say, the data relating to an earlier enquiry before you display the results of the next one. The thing to watch is that you do not erase a message before the user has had a chance to read it. You could, for example, position the ERASE just before the FIND command, so that either the result of the enquiry or the "Not Found" message is displayed on a clear screen and remains there while the program sets itself up for the next "Enter Title" request. Another method consists of erasing the previous screen completely before resuming at the DO WHILE command, but not doing so until the user signals that he is ready. This method, which may be seen in the above command file, uses the WAIT command. This command does exactly that: it displays the message "WAITING" and then waits until you press a key, any key, before it allows the program to continue. In the above example, the previous display will remain on the screen until the user presses a key, at which point the screen will clear and a fresh "Enter Title" prompt will appear.

In our illustration, the FIND command will not succeed in finding a title which has only partly been entered, e.g. "Bleak" for "Bleak House". This is because the FIND command is operating on the Titlex memory variable which is 40 characters long and contains trailing spaces. The command would thus be looking for a match on "Bleak" followed by 35 spaces. We get around this by changing the command file slightly:

```
store trim(titlex) to titlext

find &(titlext)
```

In our "Bleak" example, the field Titlext will be 5 characters long as a consequence of using the TRIM function and FIND will thus match on any title where the first 5 characters start with the contents of the Titlext field.

Finally, this section has been as much concerned with methods of controlling the command file execution as with showing how to write an enquiry program, so we will finish with a few more points on command file control. The DO to ENDDO sequence of commands is known as a DO loop. Within the DO loop we have controlled our execution of the commands with the IF, ELSE and ENDIF commands. There is another command which may be used to return to the DO command without executing any further commands. This is the LOOP command which simply stops execution at the point where it is encountered and returns to the most recent DO command. The DO and ENDDO pair may, of course, be used more than once – for example, within the main DO loop to control a sub-set of commands.

Pictures

So far, a field displayed by either the SAY or the GET clause of the @ command has been comparatively straightforward. If the field is part of a database, it looks exactly as you defined it at the CREATE stage. If it is a memory variable, it is either a character field which contains exactly what you stored to it, or it is a numeric field which is 10 positions long. Let us not forget the logical fields which are always one character in size, but display as 3 characters (e.g. .T. or .Y.) to differentiate them from ordinary fields.

What if you wanted to show a numeric value as 9,999,999 instead of 9999999? Or you might want to GET a date in such a way that the user will enter it in the correct form, for example:

: / / :

The above will quickly make it clear to the user that you do not want the date as 6 June 1984 but as 06/06/84.

The method of adding extra characters to an output field, or formatting an input field, uses certain formatting characters as part of a USING or PICTURE clause. USING accompanies SAY, while PICTURE accompanies GET. Let us look at an example:

@ 5,10 say "Enter Cost" get costx picture "9999.99"

The display resulting from the above would look like this:

Enter Cost :   0.00:

The PICTURE "9999.99" would also prevent anyone from entering an alphabetic character. A 9 specifies that only numerics may be entered. They may be accompanied by a plus or minus sign, and even by stops or commas. The format character which performs an equivalent function for alphabetic characters is "A". For example:

@ 5,10 say "Enter Supplier Code" get supcodex picture "AA"

The above will prevent the user from entering a numeric. It will, however, accept lower-case as well as upper-case alphabetic characters. Another PICTURE character which you may find useful is the exclamation mark (!), which will convert any lower-case character to upper-case. If, therefore, you specify:

```
@ 5,10 say "Enter Title" get titlex picture;
"!!!!!!!!!!!!!!!!!!!!!!!"
```

and you enter "War and Peace", you will find that you are entering in upper-case even though you have not touched the shift or capitals lock keys. The exclamation mark is particularly useful when you provide a list of options to which the user responds with an alphabetic character, such as "X to Exit". Without this PICTURE, you would have to test for lower-case "x" as well as upper-case "X" since the user might respond with either.

If you want to format the GET field, you add extra characters to the picture. Thus, PICTURE "99/99/99" is often used when asking for a date. You may similarly break up an alphabetic field, e.g. PICTURE "AA/A". When the user has entered the first two characters the cursor will jump past the / to the next character. The space character is also a valid character in this context, e.g. PICTURE "AA A".

If you do not want to exclude either numeric or alphabetic characters but still want to format the GET field, you may use the "X" formatting character in place of "9" or "A". Remember that the GET field must be large enough to contain the whole picture, not just the characters you are asking the user to enter. Thus a GET field with a PICTURE "XX XX XX" has to be 8 characters in size.

SAY specifies format characters by means of the USING clause. For example:

```
@ 5,10 say cost using "999,999.99"
```

The above will print 334 as 334.00 and 6424.75 as 6,424,75. Another feature which is useful when printing cheques is to fill in the leading zeros with asterisks. For example:

```
@ 5,10 say cost using "******.99"
```

That will print 34.50 as ****34.50. The $ sign may be used similarly, but not the £ sign.

Alphabetic fields may be formatted with "X". For example:

```
store "ABCD" TO char
@ 9,1 say char using "XX   XX"
```

will print as "AB   CD". This facility is useful for printing page headings which contain details obtained from the user or from a database record. If, say, you wanted to print three fields as part of a page heading, you could use format characters:

```
store "ABC"   to char1
store "DEFG"  to char2
store "HIJKL" to char3
@ 1,0 say char1+char2+char3 using "XXX    XXXX    XXXXX"
```

The above will produce ABC   DEFG   HIJKL. If you expect to use the same page heading layout more than once in different commands, it will be easier if you store the format characters to a memory variable and use the name of the memory variable in the @ SAY command:

```
store "'   XXX    XXXX    XXXXX'" to pic
store "ABC" to char1
store "DEFG" to char2
```

```
store "HIJKL" to char3
@ 1,0 say char1+char2+char3 using &pic
```

The above will produce:

    ABC   DEFG   HIJKL

Note that the name of the memory variable has been prefixed with the macro substitute character (&), and that the quote marks which normally delimit the USING field had to be stored into the memory variable as well. We also used two different kinds of quote marks to differentiate between those required by the STORE command and those which are to be stored.

Chapter Eight
Programming Your Work

Updating from the screen

While we have some powerful commands to edit our database and the APPEND command is simplicity in itself, you will need to provide a means of updating the database which will fit in with your other command files and which can be used by the non-technical person.

To illustrate how this is done, we will take our supplier file and write two programs. One is to add a new supplier, and the other is to edit the record of an existing supplier – such as for a change of address.

Just to remind you, the fields of the supplier file that we will be updating look like this:

```
STRUCTURE FOR FILE:   SUPPLIER.DBF
NUMBER OF RECORDS:    00173
DATE OF LAST UPDATE:  10/10/84
PRIMARY USE DATABASE
FLD        NAME       TYPE  WIDTH   DEC
001        CODE       C     002
002        NAME       C     035
003        ADDR1      C     035
004        ADDR2      C     035
005        ADDR3      C     035
006        ADDR4      C     035
007        PHONE      C     010
```

We will begin by adding a new supplier: it is the simpler of the two operations. The framework of the command file looks like this:

```
use supplier index suppind
erase
do while T
enddo
```

That gives us the structure of the program, and the ERASE command will clear the screen before we start. All we have to do now is to supply

92 *Working With dBase II*

a screen which will obtain the details of the new supplier, write those details to the database, and keep testing to see if the user wants to escape from the DO WHILE T condition.

You are already familiar with setting up one or more memory variables to receive keyboard input as part of the @ SAY GET command. Let us do that next:

```
store "  " to codex
store "                              " to namex
store namex to addr1x,addr2x,addr3x,addr4x
store "            " to phonex
@ 1,30  say "ADD A SUPPLIER"
@ 5,0   say "Supplier Code      " get codex
@ 7,0   say "Supplier Name      " get namex
@ 9,0   say "Address  Line 1    " get addr1x
@ 11,0  say "Address  Line 2    " get addr2x
@ 13,0  say "Address  Line 3    " get addr3x
@ 15,0  say "Address  Line 4    " get addr4x
@ 17,0  say "Telephone Number   " get phonex
read
if codex = "  "
   return
endif
```

Since each of the address lines is the same size as the name field, we have used the Namex memory variable to initialise the four address memory variables. The above also contains the test which will result in ending the program if the user enters a blank supplier code, i.e. if he does not want to continue the program. Assuming, however, that the READ command has left us with the details of the new supplier in our set of memory variables, we now need to write those details to the database. We cannot use the APPEND command because that will clear the screen and present the user with an empty data entry screen. Nor can we use the INSERT command because that will have the same effect. What we need is one of the editing commands which will allow us to replace existing data with new data, e.g. that which we have stored away in our memory variables. Unfortunately, you cannot edit a record which does not yet exist.

APPEND BLANK

What you do is to add an empty record with APPEND BLANK. This command not only does not produce a data entry screen since all fields are blank or empty anyway, but also sets the current record pointer to the new record so that you may edit with, say, the REPLACE command:

Programming Your Work 93

```
append blank
replace code with codex, name with namex, addr1 with addr1x;
    addr2 with addr2x, addr3 with addr3x; addr4 with addr4x;
    phone with phonex
```

Note the way in which a long command is broken into two or more lines with the semicolon. The command file described thus far is incomplete in that it will allow someone to add a supplier a second time, i.e. one that already exists on the supplier file. What we need to do is to carry out a test on the supplier code before adding the details. For example:

```
find &codex
if #<>0
   @ 23,0 say "Supplier "+codex+" already on file"
else
```

The complete command file is as follows:

```
set talk off
use supplier index suppind
erase
do while T
   store "  " to codex
   store "                              " to namex
   store namex to addr1x,addr2x,addr3x,addr4x
   store "          " to phonex
   @ 1,30  say "ADD A SUPPLIER"
   @ 5,0   say "Supplier Code        " get codex
   @ 7,0   say "Supplier Name        " get namex
   @ 9,0   say "Address Line 1       " get addr1x
   @ 11,0  say "Address Line 2       " get addr2x
   @ 13,0  say "Address Line 3       " get addr3x
   @ 15,0  say "Address Line 4       " get addr4x
   @ 17,0  say "Telephone Number     " get phonex
   read
   if codex = "  "
      erase
      return
   endif
   if #<>0
      @ 23,0 say "Supplier "+codex+" already on file"
   else
      append blank
      replace code with codex,name with namex,addr1 with addr1x;
          addr2 with addr2x,addr3 with addr3x,addr4 with addr4x;
          phone with phonex
      erase
   endif
enddo
```

94 Working With dBase II

Editing an existing supplier is slightly more complicated but follows similar lines. We start with the same framework:

```
use supplier index suppind
erase
do while T
enddo
```

We start off by asking the user to provide the code for the supplier to be edited. We then test the reply to see whether the user wants to leave the program:

```
@ 1,30   say "SUPPLIER EDIT"
store "  " to codex
@ 5,0    say "Enter Supplier Code   " get codex
read
if codex="  "
   erase
   return
else
```

If a supplier code has been entered, we follow the ELSE command with the commands which will begin by attempting to find the supplier on the database. If not found, the program will report it as "Not Found". Otherwise, the current details are stored into memory variables ready for displaying them to the user to be amended. The ERASE command clears the screen, and then the memory variables (with their current record contents) are displayed:

```
find &codex
if #=0
   @ 11,1 say "Supplier "+codex+" Not Found"
else
   store code  to codex
   store name  to namex
   store addr1 to addr1x
   store addr2 to addr2x
   store addr3 to addr3x
   store addr4 to addr4x
   store phone to phonex
   erase
   @ 1,30   say "EDIT A SUPPLIER"
   @ 5,0    say "Supplier Code        " get codex
   @ 7,0    say "Supplier Name        " get namex
   @ 9,0    say "Address  Line 1      " get addr1x
   @ 11,0   say "Address  Line 2      " get addr2x
```

```
@ 13,0   say "Address  Line 3       "  get addr3x
@ 15,0   say "Address  Line 4       "  get addr4x
@ 17,0   say "Telephone Number      "  get phonex
```
Since we have used GET to display them, as opposed to SAY, the user may edit the details as they appear on the screen. The usual editing rules apply (e.g. CTRL and X to move down, CTRL and D to move to the right, etc.) but since we are providing a service to the non-technical user it may be better to restrict them to the use of three controls:

- Return to move on a field.
- CTRL and E to move back a field.
- CTRL and C to finish before the final field has been reached.

Whether the editing is completed by CTRL and C or by pressing the Return key until the last field has been passed, the program will next READ the screen details and use them to REPLACE the existing information:

```
read
replace name with namex, addr1 with addr1x;
        addr2 with addr2x, addr3 with addr3x;
        addr4 with addr4x, phone with phonex
```

The complete command file is as follows:

```
set talk off
use supplier index suppind
erase
do while T
  @ 1,30  say "SUPPLIER EDIT"
  store "  " to codex
  @ 5,0   say "Enter Supplier Code   " get codex
  read
  if codex="  "
  erase
  return
else
  find &codex
  if #=0
    @ 11,1 say "Supplier "+codex+" Not Found"
  else
    store code   to codex
    store name   to namex
    store addr1  to addr1x
    store addr2  to addr2x
```

```
            store addr3 to addr3x
            store addr4 to addr4x
            store phone to phonex
            erase
            @ 1,30   say "EDIT A SUPPLIER"
            @ 5,0    say "Supplier Code        :"+codex
            @ 7,0    say "Supplier Name        " get namex
            @ 9,0    say "Address    Line 1    " get addr1x
            @ 11,0   say "Address    Line 2    " get addr2x
            @ 13,0   say "Address    Line 3    " get addr3x
            @ 15,0   say "Address    Line 4    " get addr4x
            @ 17,0   say "Telephone Number     " get phonex
            read
            replace name with namex, addr1 with addr1x;
                    addr2 with addr2x, addr3 with addr3x;
                    addr4 with addr4x, phone with phonex
            erase
          endif
        endif
enddo
```

We have not allowed the user to change the supplier code itself because it is used as a link to our BOOKS file, and changing it would disturb the relationship between the two files.

Format files

A format file provides you with a means of storing your @ commands in a separate file and calling them up as required. Such files are identified by the suffix .FMT. For example:

BOOKS.FMT

The reason for providing this facility is that you may find yourself in a position of being able to use the same set of @ commands in more than one command file. It is convenient, in such a situation, to be able to store these common commands in a file which may be brought into and become part of your command file as you are executing it. You do this by adding the SET FORMAT TO command to your command file and using the READ command to bring in the @ commands from the format file. The content of the format file will be read from disk and displayed as part of the READ command provided that you have previously issued the SET FORMAT TO command in respect of that format file. For example:

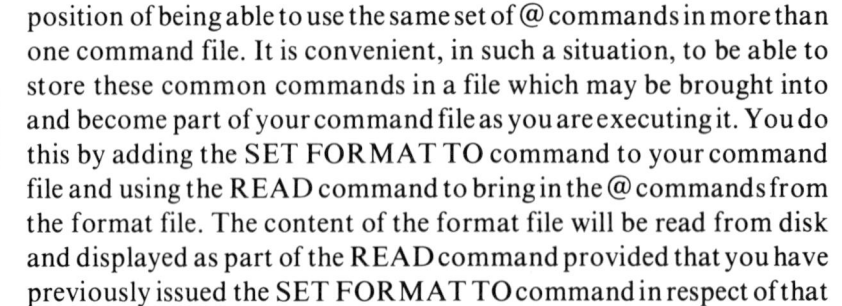

```
    set format to books
```

The suffix .FMT will automatically be added by dBase II before it starts to look for the file.

There is no difference between the @ commands which you may have had in your command file, and those which you call from a format file. You may use either as it suits you. Only @ commands and * commands may be contained in a format file. The following is an example:

```
*     books format file   (BOOKS.FMT)
@ 5,0    say "Title              "  get titlex
@ 7,0    say "Author             "  get authorx
@ 9,0    say "Classification     "  get classx
@ 11,0   say "Supplier Code      "  get supcodex
@ 13,0   say "No. Copies Bought  "  get noboughtx
@ 15,0   say "Cost               "  get costx
@ 17,0   say "Shops              "  get shopsx
@ 19,0   say "Number Sold        "  get nosoldx
@ 21,0   say "Sales Value        "  get pricex
```

MODIFY COMM- AND

A format file may be edited with the dBase II editor. For example:

```
    .modify command books.fmt
```

Remember to supply the .FMT suffix, otherwise dBase II will assume a suffix of .CMD (or .PRG on 16-bit computers). As an alternative, you may use any word processor or text editor.

The following is an example of using the format file in a program which provides an editing screen to enable a user to update the BOOKS database:

```
* EDIT A BOOK RECORD
set talk off
use books index titles
erase
do while T
  @ 1,30  say "BOOKS EDIT"
  store "                                           " to titlex
  @ 5,0   say "Enter Title    " get titlex
  read
  if titlex=" "
    erase
    return
  else
    find &titlex
    if #=0
      @ 11,1 say titlex+" Not Found"
    else
      store title   to titlex
      store author  to authorx
```

98 Working With dBase II

```
            store class      to classx
            store supcode    to supcodex
            store nobought   to noboughtx
            store cost       to costx
            store shops      to shopsx
            store nosold     to nosoldx
            store price      to pricex
            erase
            set format to books
            read
            set format to screen
            replace title with titlex,author with authorx,class with classx;
               supcode with supcodex,nobought with noboughtx,cost with costx;
               shops with shopsx,nosold with nosoldx,price with pricex
            erase
         endif
      endif
enddo
```

Although we are here dealing with a different database, and the @ commands have disappeared, you will recognise that the command file structure is a duplicate of that used for editing the suppliers' file. Similarly, in the command file which provides a means of adding a new title to the BOOKS database, the major difference is the replacement of a large number of @ commands with a single SET FORMAT TO command:

```
* ADD A BOOK RECORD
set talk off
use books index titles
do while T
   store "                          " to titlex
   store "                     " to authorx
   store "        " to classx
   store "  " to supcodex
   store 0 to noboughtx,nosoldx
   store 0.00 to costx,pricex
   store "       " to shopsx
   erase
   set format to books
   read
   set format to screen
   if titlex=" "
     return
   endif
   append blank
   replace title with titlex,author with authorx,class with classx;
      supcode with supcodex,nobought with noboughtx,cost with costx;
      shops with shopsx
enddo
```

You will notice that as soon as the READ command has been issued, the SET FORMAT TO command is used again, this time to the screen. The reason is that SET commands remain in force until you cancel them or until you leave dBase II with the QUIT command. Thus, the READ command will continue to look for, and use, the @

Programming Your Work **99**

commands contained in the most recently specified format file until the SET FORMAT TO SCREEN cancels the instruction. Until such time, any @ commands contained in the command file will be displayed but will be so quickly overwritten by those from the Format file that you will hardly have time to register them.

Creating a menu

By answering no more than the most basic requirements (e.g. producing a report, providing screen enquiries, and updating files), we are already dealing with a number of command files. Provided we give them names which are easily remembered, we could hand them over to our users and expect the users to get on with it. Alternatively, we could go a step further and provide a menu so that our users would be required to do no more than select an option from amongst several. For example:

```
List Books by Supplier
Title Enquiry
Add a Supplier
Edit a Supplier
Add a Title (Book)
Edit a Title (Book)
```

The user should be able to load dBase II and DO a single command file which would present him with a menu containing the above as a list of options. He would then simply indicate his choice and the appropriate command file would be loaded without any further effort on his part. When he had finished using that command file, he would be taken automatically back to the menu from which he would select the next option.

Let us start by using what we already know:

```
set talk off
do while T
   erase
   store " " to option
   @ 1,30 say "GOOD BOOKS COMPANY"
   @ 5,0  say "1. List Books by Supplier"
   @ 6,0  say "2. Title Enquiry"
   @ 7,0  say "3. Add a Supplier"
   @ 8,0  say "4. Edit a Supplier"
   @ 9,0  say "5. Add a Title"
   @ 10,0 say "6. Edit a Title"
   @ 11,0 say "X. Exit"
   @ 13,0 say "Enter your choice" get option;
                              picture "!"
```

```
    read
    if option = "X"
       erase
       return
    endif
    if option = "1"
       do supbooks
    endif
    if option = "2"
       do bookenq
    endif
    if option = "3"
       do addsupp
    endif
    if option = "4"
       do editsupp
    endif
    if cption = "5"
       do addbook
    endif
    if option = "6"
       do editbook
    endif
 enddo
```

Any DO command in this command file will bring in and execute another command file. This will then return to where it left off: this command file and continue with the rest of the commands. There is a limit to the number of DOs which may be made in this way, i.e. command file 1 calling command file 2, which calls command file 3, etc., until the control eventually returns to command file 1. The term for this is *nested*, i.e. each command file is 'nested' within the one that calls it with the DO command. The limit imposed is not on nesting itself, but on the number of files which may be opened at any one time including the database in use, i.e. 16. Assuming that only a single file is in USE – no indexes, etc. – you may nest up to 15 command files.

Having covered the technical limits, let us return to the menu command file. You will notice that it has a long list of IF and ENDIF commands. There is a more attractive way of doing the same thing by using the DO CASE version of the DO command:

```
    set talk off
    do while T
       erase
```

Programming Your Work

```
store " " to option
@ 1,30 say "GOOD BOOKS COMPANY"
@ 5,0  say "1. List Books by Supplier"
@ 6,0  say "2. Title Enquiry"
@ 7,0  say "3. Add a Supplier"
@ 8,0  say "4. Edit a Supplier"
@ 9,0  say "5. Add a Title"
@ 10,0 say "6. Edit a Title"
@ 11,0 say "X. Exit"
@ 13,0 say "Enter your choice" get option;
                              picture "!"
read
do case
   case option = "X"
      erase
      return
   case option = "1"
      do supbooks
   case option = "2"
      do bookenq
   case option = "3"
      do addsupp
   case option = "4"
      do editsupp
   case option = "5"
      do addbook
   case option = "6"
      do editbook
   endcase
enddo
```

The commands following the CASE line which is true, will be executed up to before the next CASE line. The program will then resume at the command which follows the ENDCASE command. If none of the CASE lines are true, the program will ignore them all and move to the command after the ENDCASE.

You may also use the OTHERWISE statement. For example:

```
case option = "5"
     do addbook
otherwise
     do editbook
endcase
```

In this situation, if none of the CASE lines are true, the command(s) following the OTHERWISE command will be executed.

As we are calling several command files, each of which could be using @ GET commands, you should be aware of a dBase II restriction on the number of @ GET commands in use. A maximum of 64 GETs may be active at one time. None of the command files we have created so far are likely to cause difficulties since we have used the ERASE command each time before leaving the command file. ERASE not only clears the screen, but also the memory allocated to the storage of details obtained through the @ GET command. Another command which may be used to clear the memory allocated to such details but which does not clear the screen, is the CLEAR GETS command. Be careful, however, not to use the CLEAR command on its own since it resets dBase II completely by closing all files.

Let us look at two more screen handling methods. Hitherto we have used the @ GET command to ask the user for information. There are two other commands which may be used in the same way: INPUT and ACCEPT. Both perform the function of displaying data and receiving the user's response, which is stored into the specified memory variable. For example:

    input "Enter your choice" to option

    accept "Enter your choice" to option

The difference lies in the fact that ACCEPT will only operate on character fields so that whatever the user enters will be in a character memory variable. INPUT will determine the type of variable from the type of data the user enters. For example:

    49.56 will result in a numeric variable

    "Dickens" will result in a character variable

    T (or Y,F,etc.) will result in a logical variable

With INPUT the user has to surround a character field with quote marks; with ACCEPT there is no need. Indeed ACCEPT would store the quote marks as part of the character field.

Neither command needs the READ command since they will take care of the transfer of data from the screen to the specified memory variable. The data to be displayed is optional – the following would do just as well:

    input to option

    accept to option

These commands are convenient to use and will often be seen in command files, but remember that they are unable to control the entry of data in the way that the @ GET command does with the PICTURE clause.

So far, we have used the RETURN command to leave a command file. Another command, very similar to RETURN, will also return to the dot prompt. This is the CANCEL command. Whereas RETURN will leave the current command file and return either to the command file which called it with a DO command or to the dot prompt, CANCEL will cancel all commands files and return directly to the dot prompt.

Finally, since we are leaving the menu, we should also ensure that all files have been closed. We will, therefore, add an extra command to the exit routine:

    case option = "X"
      erase
      clear
      return

The CLEAR command will release all memory variables and close all files so that the next menu can start with a clean slate. The CLEAR command is often used at the beginning of a menu command file for this very reason.

Name and address labels

One of the distinct advantages of using a computer is that it takes over doing the most tedious jobs. One of these must be the task of typing names and addresses on envelopes when you are sending out promotional material. Let us see how we would use dBase II to do the job for us.

We are going to write to all our credit customers who have not made any purchases during the past three months. Just to remind ourselves, we will first have a look at the structure of the CUSTOMER file:

    STRUCTURE FOR FILE: CUSTOMER.DBF
    NUMBER OF RECORDS: 00482

```
DATE OF LAST UPDATE: 11/11/84
PRIMARY USE DATABASE
FLD        NAME          TYPE  WIDTH    DEC
001        CUSTCODE       C     005
002        SURNAME        C     035
003        TITLE          C     005
004        INITIALS       C     008
005        ADDR1          C     035
006        ADDR2          C     035
007        ADDR3          C     035
008        ADDR4          C     035
009        PHONE          C     010
010        DATE           C     006
011        NOSOLD         N     005
012        PRICE          N     010      002
```

We are going to order special continuous stationery which contains blank adhesive labels, and print on those instead of typing envelopes. Usually the labels are positioned side by side so that you have two or three abreast. We are ordering the former. Our command file will thus have to store the first customer's details until the second customer record has been read so that one print line will contain both names, or both first address lines, etc. We will leave until later the method of selecting customer records according to the age of their last purchase, and concentrate for now on producing the adhesive labels.

The method consists of using an indicator which tells you whether you should place the next name and address into position for the first label or for the second (or third if there are three abreast). We are going to use the logical memory variable Right as an indicator to tell us whether we should move the name and address to the first or second label. It will be false for the left-most label position, and true for the right-most position. Of course, we will have to set and reset the contents of the logical memory variable ourselves as we go along. Let us look at part of the command file:

```
use customer
store N to right
do while .not. eof
  if .not. right
    store trim(title)+" "+trim(initials)+" "+trim(surname) to left1
    store addr1 to left2
    store addr2 to left3
    store addr3 to left4
    store addr4 to left5
    store Y to right
  else
    store trim(title)+" "+trim(initials)+" "+trim(surname) to right1
```

```
          store addr1 to right2
          store addr2 to right3
          store addr3 to right4
          store addr4 to right5
          store N to right
        endif
        skip
      enddo
      return
```

Note the following:

● The use of the TRIM function to discard superfluous trailing spaces, and the addition of single spaces to separate fields.

● The alternating contents of the Right memory variable which is set each time to reflect the next free label position.

Having set up two names and addresses, we have to print them. The problem is that the page length is equal to the number of lines there are between the top of one label and the next one down. So we either set our printer up to use short pages, e.g. 8 lines each, or we use a line count method such as that described in Chapter 7, in 'Programming a report'. Another method would have been available but for our use of the TRIM function: the ? command ignores page boundaries and is perfectly suited to the production of labels. Unfortunately, the use of the TRIM function results in a variable length field (depending on the number of trailing spaces which have been removed), so that printing becomes uncertain. Let us see what happens when we use the results of the above command file extract with the ? command. For example:

```
      ? left1,right1
      ? left2,right2
      ? left3,right3
      ? left4,right4
      ? left5,right5
      Mr. A.A. James Miss P. James
      24 Bedford Hall,           Mia Casa,
      235 Front Street,          56 Cliff Road,
      Middle Town.               High Town.
```

TRIM has moved the second name up close to the first name. The address lines, however, remain spaced out because the full field lengths are used. To avoid this happening, we are going to use the @ SAY command and set the printer to a short page equivalent to the label depth:

```
set print on
set format to print
set talk off
use customer
```

```
store N to right
do while .not. eof
  if .not. right
    store trim(title)+" "+trim(initials)+" "+trim(surname) to left1
    store addr1 to left2
    store addr2 to left3
    store addr3 to left4
    store addr4 to left5
    store Y to right
  else
    store trim(title)+" "+trim(initials)+" "+trim(surname) to right1
    store addr1 to right2
    store addr2 to right3
    store addr3 to right4
    store addr4 to right5
    store N to right
    @ 0,1 say left1
    @ 0,40 say right1
    @ 1,1 say left2
    @ 1,40 say right2
    @ 2,1 say left3
    @ 2,40 say right3
    @ 3,1 say left4
    @ 3,40 say right4
    @ 4,1 say left5
    @ 4,40 say right5
  endif
  skip
endif
enddo
eject
set print off
set talk on
set format to screen
return
```

This will produce labels as below. Note the fact that some labels contain more lines than others, but remain positioned correctly.

Mr. A.A. James   Miss P. James
24 Bedford Hall,   Mia Casa,
235 Front Street,   56 Cliff Road,
Middle Town.   High Town.

Mr. M.H. James   Mrs. D.F. Jason
24 North Drive,   Town House,
Middle Town.   Town Square,
                                        Middle Town.

Dr. J.P. Maxwell   Miss L.H. Longman
The Meadow,   15 Scenic Drive,
17 Hill Top,   Middle Town.
Middle Town.

Suppose, however, that we had an uneven number of records on the file. What would happen to the final record? We will have to insert a final test after the ENDDO command just in case there is a name and address which remains to be printed:

```
enddo
if right
   @ 0,1 say left1
   @ 1,1 say left2
   @ 2,1 say left3
   @ 3,1 say left4
   @ 4,1 say left5
endif
eject
set print off
set talk on
set format to screen
return
```

We might want to add the following at the front of the command file to obtain a date from the user which will be used to test against the last purchase date on each customer's record:

```
erase
@ i,30 say "Customer Selection"
store "      " to datex
@ 5,1 say "Enter Cut-off Date in form YYMMDD" get datex picture "999999"
read
```

Finally, we will add a date test to the command file:

```
do while .not. eof
if date > datex
   skip
else
```

The complete command file is given below:

```
erase
@ i,30 say "Customer Selection"
store "      " to datex
@ 5,1 say "Enter Cut-off Date in form YYMMDD" get datex picture "999999"
read
set print on
set format to print
set talk off
use customer
store N to right
do while .not. eof
   if date > datex
```

```
      skip
    else
      if .not. right
        store trim(title)+" "+trim(initials)+" "+trim(surname) to left1
        store addr1 to left2
        store addr2 to left3
        store addr3 to left4
        store addr4 to left5
        store Y to right
      else
        store trim(title)+" "+trim(initials)+" "+trim(surname) to right1
        store addr1 to right2
        store addr2 to right3
        store addr3 to right4
        store addr4 to right5
        store N to right
        @ 0,1 say left1
        @ 0,40 say right1
        @ 1,1 say left2
        @ 1,40 say right2
        @ 2,1 say left3
        @ 2,40 say right3
        @ 3,1 say left4
        @ 3,40 say right4
        @ 4,1 say left5
        @ 4,40 say right5
      endif
      skip
    endif
enddo
if right
  @ 0,1 say left1
  @ 1,1 say left2
  @ 2,1 say left3
  @ 3,1 say left4
  @ 4,1 say left5
endif
eject
set print off
set talk on
set format to screen
return
```

We will now turn our attention to the promotional material that is being sent to the customers. It consists of publishers' leaflets and a letter from us. The letter could be preprinted with a standard 'Dear Sir or Madam', or we could use dBase II to print the name of each customer, like 'Dear Miss Jones', or even to print the whole letter to give it a more personal touch.

If we decide to print the name only, we will order preprinted continuous stationery containing all but the name. This will be fed into the printer and lined up so that the first line to be printed coincides with the top of the form, and is positioned where we want the 'Dear ....'. The command file is not very different from that used for the name and address labels. The controlling section looks like this:

```
do while .not.eof
  if date > datex
    skip
  else
    ? "Dear ",trim(title),surname
    eject
    skip
  endif
enddo
```

The EJECT command will throw the paper to the next top of form which will, of course, be where we want the next 'Dear . . . .' to be printed.

To print the whole letter, we simply expand the command file to contain the text of the letter by following the ? command which prints the name with further ? commands containing the text of each line. Use the ? command on its own for space between paragraphs.

Version 2.4 onwards of dBase II contains a new command, TEXT, which makes this job even easier. Any text which appears between the TEXT command and its companion ENDTEXT will be displayed, so you could, for example, follow the ? command which prints the name with the command TEXT, then the text of the letter, followed by the ENDTEXT command. If you want a longer text line than the screen will allow, use a semi-colon at the end of a line to join it to the next line.

A common approach to using this method is to prepare the text of the letter on a word processor, and then copy it into the command file (see Appendix B). The advantage of the TEXT command is that you do not have to surround each line with quote marks, nor prefix it with the ? command.

Chapter Nine
Going Further

Macro substitution

We have so far used the macro substitute character (&) with the FIND command to tell the latter that we want it to find the contents of the field which has been prefixed with the &. For example:

    find &titlex

In a way, this may not seem very different from other commands which use memory variables. For example:

    @ 1,30 say title

will not print the word 'title' but the contents of the field Title. Let us see what happens if we do the following:

    . store "books" to dname
    books
    . use dname
    FILE DOES NOT EXIST

dBase II tried to find a file called DNAME. It did not look for the contents of a field called Dname. Now try it again as follows:

    . store "books" to dname
    books
    . use &dname

It worked that time. The difference lies in the fact that certain commands are designed to use memory variables, and others are not. The macro substitute character allows you to bring in the contents of a field and use it as a part of a command. It is as if the command line passes through a preliminary process whereby any words which are prefixed with an & are replaced by the contents of the fields referenced by those words. Let us look at the example given at the beginning of this chapter:

    find &titlex

Going Further

The substitution process will look for the field Titlex, and use its contents to replace the word &titlex, resulting in:

```
find As You Like It
```

Then dBase II will execute the command. An entire command may be replaced in this way. For example:

```
. store "list author,title off" to command
. &command
Shakespeare            As You Like It
Dickens                Bleak House
Tolstoy                War and Peace
```

Macro substitution is a very powerful processing tool. Let us look at it being used to look up tables of information. For the purposes of this illustration, we will assume that our stock file BOOKS no longer contains the price of each book but has a price code instead, e.g. Price Code A = 1.99, Price Code B = 2.50, etc. The fieldname in the database is no longer Price, but Pricecode. We now want to perform a What If? exercise to determine the amount by which our stock would increase in sales value if we decide to change the price range.

Our program will first ask for the current price range:

```
set talk off
erase
input "Enter Old Price for Code A " to old:a
input "                         B " to old:b
input "                         C " to old:c
```

Next we will ask for the proposed price range:

```
?
?
input "Enter New Price for Code A " to new:a
input "                         B " to new:b
input "                         C " to new:c
```

Look closely at the fieldnames given to the memory variables which are being used to store the prices. Each fieldname has been carefully selected to contain, as part of the fieldname, the price code which the field represents. Now what do we want the program to do? After reading a record, it should use the price code to look up two tables, the original prices and the proposed prices, and extract the old and new prices for that price code. This is where macro substitution helps us:

112 *Working With dBase II*

```
use books
do while .not. eof
  store "old:"+pricecode to j
  store &j to oldprice
  store "new:"+pricecode to j
  store &j to newprice
  skip
enddo
```

The first STORE puts the characters OLD: plus the price code from the first record into a field called J. If the price code of the first record is B, then J will contain OLD:B which, of course, is the name of the second of the memory variables containing the current prices. So all we have to do now is to use the contents of J in another STORE command to get at the current price for price code B:

```
store &j to oldprice
```

Then we set J up again to contain the fieldname of the memory variable which contains the proposed price for price code B, and use &J to obtain that figure. There is nothing special about calling the field J. It could equally well have been called Field or Pointer or some other name of your choice.

Let us look at a complete program which does a What If? pricing exercise on our stock of novels. It will print each Title, the price code, the old price and the proposed price. It will also give the total stock value at the old prices and at the proposed prices, and show the increase in value.

```
set talk off
erase
input "Enter Old Price for Code A " to old:a
input "                           B " to old:b
input "                           C " to old:c
?
?
input "Enter New Price for Code A " to new:a
input "                           B " to new:b
input "                           C " to new:c
store 0 to oldtot,newtot
set print on
set format to print
@ 10,46 say "Old Price"
@ 10,57 say "New Price"
store 12 to lines
```

Going Further **113**

```
use books
do while .not. eof
  if class="Novel"
    store "old:"+pricecode to j
    store &j to oldprice
    store "new:"+pricecode to j
    store &j to newprice
    store oldtot + oldprice to oldtot
    store newtot + newprice to newtot
    @ lines,1 say title
    @ lines,43 say pricecode
    @ lines,45 say oldprice
    @ lines,56 say newprice
    store lines + 1 to lines
  endif
  skip
enddo
store lines + 1 to lines
@ lines,45 say oldtot
@ lines,56 say newtot
store lines + 2 to lines
@ lines,4 say "Increase = "
store newtot - oldtot to diff
@ lines,20 say diff
eject
set print off
set format to screen
set talk on
```

The result will look like this:

```
Enter Old Price for Band A :1.99
                          B :2.50
                          C :3.75


Enter New Price for Band A :2.25
                          B :2.99
                          C :3.99

                             Old Price   New Price

Pride and Prejudice    B        2.50        2.99
Dombey and Son         B        2.50        2.99
Treasure Island        A        1.99        2.25
```

Turn of the Screw	B	2.50	2.99
Far from the Madding Crowd	C	3.75	3.99
War and Peace	C	3.75	3.99
Bleak House	B	2.50	2.99
Crime and Punishment	B	2.50	2.99
		21.99	25.18

```
    Increase  =             3.19
```

You may like to add a few extra commands to direct the information to the printer.

Memory variables

There have already been several examples of the use of memory variables, but they have so far been restricted to acting as temporary fields in the processing of a screen display, or a calculation, etc. We are now going to look at three commands which extend their use considerably.

You may remember from the chapter on counting and totalling that you may only have 64 memory variables at any one time. Memory variables are global, i.e. they do not belong to a single command file but may be accessed by any command file that has been called by the user. You do not have 64 per command file, but 64 over all command files. This could create a problem for someone who has set up a sophisticated menu system which runs a number of different command files, each of which employs several memory variables. What do you do when you need to use the 65th memory variable?

Memory variables are not cancelled by the RETURN command; they remain allocated until you QUIT the session, issue the CLEAR command, or until you release their allocation with the RELEASE command. This command operates in several forms. The simplest is:

```
    release titlex
```

In this case, a single memory variable is released. The same form of the RELEASE command may be used to release a list of memory variables. Alternatively, you could release all memory variables:

```
    .release titlex,authorx
```

or

```
release all
```

The ALL clause may be qualified by two kinds of skeleton or part specification. The first is one which is similar to that employed by CP/M and DOS, i.e. the use of ? or * in the name, thus:

```
release all like book*
```

The above would release all memory variables beginning with the letters BOOK. The alternative form:

```
release all like book??x
```

would release all memory variables beginning with BOOK and ending in X but having any other two characters in between. The asterisk is used to accept any number of characters following the specified characters, while the question marks accept any embedded characters.

The second type of skeleton clause which qualifies the RELEASE command is the opposite of the first:

```
release all except book*
```

or

```
release all except book??x
```

Now that we have discovered how to control the allocation of memory variables, let us consider how we may extend their use. There is a dBase II command called SAVE which will write all current memory variables to a disk file. There is another command called RESTORE which will restore them from disk back to memory. You could have several different sets of memory variables on disk, because when you SAVE or RESTORE you specify the filename of the disk file containing the variables. The latter is suffixed with the letters .MEM to distinguish it from other files. For example:

```
save to books
```

The above will write the current memory variables to a file called BOOKS.MEM. If the file does not exist it will be created. The SAVE command is able to operate selectively with the ALL LIKE clause, much as the RELEASE command does. For example:

```
save to books all like book*
```

or

```
save to books all like book??x
```

RESTORE specifies the file from which the memory variables are to be read. For example:

```
restore from books
```

RESTORE The thing to remember with the RESTORE command is that it will delete all the memory variables which may have been created by earlier commands, i.e. it will overwrite all current memory variables. Version 2.4 provides you with the means of avoiding this by specifying that the incoming memory variables are added to existing ones rather than overwriting them. This is done with the ADDITIVE clause. For example:

```
restore from books additive
```

A good reason for using the SAVE and RESTORE commands is that it gives you flexibility. If you do want to use a large number of memory variables in a command file and expect to clash with another command file which also requires a large number of memory variables, you could perform a RESTORE on entering the command file and a SAVE prior to leaving it. In this way you do not have to concern yourself with what is happening outside the command file itself in terms of the use of memory variables.

You may also use these commands in an alternative approach to storing data. If, for example, you maintain changing parameters such as the prices corresponding to the price codes which are stored on the database, you may not want to ask the user to re-enter the prices each time he switches on. You could, of course, create a separate database specially for such items. It is, however, far more convenient to keep that sort of information in the form that you want to use it and without having to restructure a database when it becomes necessary to add an extra memory variable.

Let us look at the What If? example from the previous section of this chapter in the light of the SAVE and RESTORE commands. First we will ask for the current prices and store them:

```
set talk off
erase
? "                    CURRENT PRICES"
?
input "Enter Old Price for Code A " to old:a
input "                           B " to old:b
input "                           C " to old:c
save to prices
```

Going Further

Then we provide a means of changing them:

```
restore from prices
erase
? "                     PRICE CHANGES"
?
@ 12,0 say "Enter Changed Price for Code A " get old:a
@ 14,0 say "                              B " get old:b
@ 16,0 say "                              C " get old:c
read
save to prices
```

We could not use the INPUT command for the price changes because it does not display the current contents of a field on the screen; it simply sets up an empty screen area for you to use to enter information. So, we used the @ GET combination instead, which will display the field as it stands and allow you to change it.

Next, we perform the What If? This time, of course, we do not have to waste the user's time by asking for current prices:

```
set talk off
erase
restore from prices
?
?
input "Enter New Price for Band A " to new:a
input "                         B " to new:b
input "                         C " to new:c
```

The rest of the command file would be identical to that given in the previous section.

Remember when you are using memory variables that you have a very useful command available to check on the number of memory variables as well as examining their content:

```
. display memory
OLD:A        (N)    1.99
OLD:B        (N)    2.99
OLD:C        (N)    3.99
** TOTAL **        03 VARIABLES USED   00018 BYTES USED
```

Preparing invoices

You will remember that back in Chapter 6 we had a database file

118 *Working With dBase II*

which contained details of each day's sales. We are now going to merge together the files representing the past week's sales, and then produce an invoice for each credit customer found on the file.

Merging the files is simple. We COPY the first file and APPEND the rest. To improve the illustration we are going to call the daily files by weekday names:

```
. use salemon
. copy to week49 for custcode#"     "
. use week49
. append from saletue for custcode#"     "
. append from salewed for custcode#"     "
. append from salethu for custcode#"     "
. append from salefri for custcode#"     "
. append from salesat for custcode#"     "
```

You will see that we have excluded cash sales by selecting only those records which contain a credit customer code. Next, we are going to index the weekly file on customer and date:

```
. index on custcode+date to weekind
```

The date is already being held in the form YYMMDD because we made that a requirement at the time of designing the structure of the sales file. The index will thus provide a file sequence which will show more than one purchase by the same customer in the correct date sequence. All we have to do now is write a program which will read the week's sales, match each customer to the customer file to obtain his or her name and address, and then use the information from the two files to print an invoice for each customer.

We start by repeating the earlier steps as part of the command file:

```
set talk off
erase
?
? "            INVOICE PREPARATION"
?
?
accept "Enter Week Number        " to weekno
?
?
? "     Which drive for            "
accept "          the weekly file?" to weekdr
accept "          the daily files?" to daydr
store weekdr+":week"+weekno to weekfile
```

Going Further

```
store daydr+":salemon" to dayfile
use &dayfile
copy to &weekfile for custcode#"     "
use &weekfile
store "tuewedthufrisat" to days
store 1 to dayno
do while dayno < 6
   store  $(dayfile,1,6)+$(days,dayno*3-2,3) to dayfile
   append from &dayfile
   store dayno + 1 to dayno
enddo
index on custcode+date to weekind
```

We ask the user to tell us the week number, on which drive the daily sales files are loaded, and where the weekly file should be created. The drive references are first combined with a colon and the rest of the filename to give us, for example, A:WEEK49 or B:SALEMON, and then inserted into the USE, COPY and APPEND commands by means of the macro substitute character (&). Having copied the first sales file to create the weekly file, we then resort to a DO loop to set up the filename for each daily sales file and APPEND it to the weekly file by repeating the DO loop five times. Note the way in which the substring function is used on a pre-set string of characters to obtain the appropriate day for each filename.

The problem with such a command file is that it relies heavily on the user to set things up correctly and to supply correct information. We should make it less dependent by adding some checks on the user. We could, for example, check that the daily sales files really are where the user said they are:

```
if .not. file(dayfile)
  ? dayfile+" not found"
```

Let us insert that into the command file and at the same time extend the DO loop to include the first daily sales file:

```
store weekdr+":week"+weekno to weekfile
store 1 to dayno
store "montuewedthufrisat" to days
do while dayno < 7
   store daydr+":sale"+$(days,dayno*3-2,3)   to dayfile
   if .not. file(dayfile)
      ? dayfile+" not found"
      ?
      accept "  Re-enter Drive or X to cancel" to daydr
```

```
   if daydr = "X" .or. daydr="x"
     erase
     return
   endif
else
   if dayno = 1
     use &dayfile
     copy to &weekfile for custcode#"     "
     use &weekfile
   else
     append from &dayfile
   endif
   store dayno + 1 to dayno
   endif
enddo
index on custcode+date to weekind
```

Having completed the creation and indexing of the weekly sales file, we may now move on to producing the invoices. The weekly file is still in USE and the index is already set, so we will next open the Customer file and set its index:

```
select secondary
use customer index custcode
select primary
restore from invno
store "      " to custcodex
set print on
```

We have also prepared two memory variables. The final invoice number from the previous invoicing run has been obtained by means of the RESTORE command. The Custcodex variable has been initialised to spaces ready to act as a comparison field to check for change of customer on the sales file. Note that the RESTORE command comes first. If it had followed the STORE command, it would have cleared the Custcodex variable (unless you had specified the ADDITIVE clause available in Version 2.4 onwards). Note also that before using the command file for the first time, you will have to set up the INVNO.MEM file by storing zero to a variable called INVNO and issuing a SAVE TO INVNO command. The above is followed with the DO loop:

Going Further

```
do while .not. eof
  if custcode#custcodex
    if custcodex#"        "
      ?
      ? "                              ",;
        "              TOTAL         ",pricetot
      ? "                              ",;
        "                             ======="
    endif
    store custcode to custcodex
    select secondary
    find &custcodex
    select primary
    store 0.00 to pricetot
    store invno + 1 to invno
    eject
    ? "                    Invoice Date   ",date()
    ?
    ? "                    Invoice Number ",str(invno,4)
    ?
    ?
    ? trim(s.title),trim(initials),surname
    ? addr1
    ? addr2
    ? addr3
    ? addr4
    ?
    ?
    ?
  endif
  ? nosold," ",title,price/nosold,price
  store pricetot + price to pricetot
  skip
enddo
?
? "                              ",;
  "              TOTAL         ",pricetot
? "                              ",;
  "                             ======="
eject
save to invno
return
```

122 *Working With dBase II*

This is what the invoices will look like:

```
                    Invoice Date    10/10/84

                    Invoice Number    31

Mr. A.A. James
24 Bedford Hall,
235 Front Street,
Middle Town.



   2    Dombey and Son                           2.35      4.70
   1    Far from the Madding Crowd              2.99      2.99

                                   TOTAL                  7.69
                                                       =======
```

```
                    Invoice Date    10/10/84

                    Invoice Number    32

Mr. M.H. James
24 North Drive,
Middle Town.



   2    Bleak House                              1.25      2.50

                                   TOTAL                  2.50
                                                       =======
```

```
                    Invoice Date    10/10/84

                    Invoice Number    33

Mr. H.A. Jameson
24 Sun Terrace
Moon Street
Middle Town


   1    War and Peace                            2.45      2.45
   2    Henry V                                  2.50      5.00
   2    As You Like It                           1.99      3.98

                                   TOTAL                 11.43
                                                       =======
```

Validating the date

Many applications require you to obtain from the user a date which will subsequently be used in a command file to test against database records, e.g. to produce an aged debtors list, or name and address labels for contacting customers who have not made any purchases for some time.

This date will be used blind – that is, you will not see it being applied to the database records since that happens inside the command file. It might, therefore, be prudent to validate such a user-supplied date before using it. The following is an example of a command file which asks for a date, validates it, and then calls the Name and Address Labels command file:

```
set talk off
erase
do while T
  @ 1,30 say "Customer Selection"
  store "      " to datex
  @ 5,1 say "Enter Date in form YYMMDD" get datex picture "999999"
  read
  if datex="000000"
    return
  endif
  store val($(datex,5,2)) to day
  store val($(datex,3,2)) to month
  store val($(datex,1,2)) to year
  store date() to dat
  store val($(dat,7,2)) to curyr
  store curyr-1 to lastyr
  store 0 to yy,mm,dd
  if year=curyr .or. year=lastyr
    store 1 to yy
  endif
  if month > 0 .and. month < 13
    store 1 to mm
  endif
  if day > 0 .and. day < 32
    store 1 to dd
  endif
  if yy=1 .and. mm=1 .and. dd=1
    do label
    return
  else
    @ 9,1 say "Invalid Date"
  endif
enddo
```

Refer to the chapter on dBase II functions if necessary, but the short description which follows will probably explain the major points:

(1) The screen is cleared and the user is asked for a date. The PICTURE clause forces numeric-only entry.

(2) The READ command transfers the date to the Datex field.

(3) The user may escape by entering six zeros in the date field.

(4) We now validate the user-supplied date:

(i) The VAL and $ functions are used together to create numeric fields containing the entered year, month, and day.

(ii) The DATE and VAL functions are used to obtain the current year and we then subract one to obtain the previous year. The latter represents the earliest year we are prepared to accept.

(iii) Next we check that the user-entered year is equal to the current year or previous year; that the month is in the range 1 to 12; and that the day is in the range 1 to 31. On each successful test we set an indicator (i.e. convert a previous setting of zero to one) to reflect the outcome of the test.

(5) When these three tests have been completed, we test the three indicators. If all three are set (i.e. contain a '1'), we call the next command file (i.e. LABEL) with the DO command. If the date had been invalid (i.e. if one of the indicators had not been set), we display a message to that effect and return to the DO WHILE command for another attempt at obtaining the cut-off date.

Note, incidentally, that if you had used STORE T TO YY, STORE T TO MM, etc., you would have concluded with a simpler final IF command, thus,

```
if yy .and. mm .and. dd
```

Alternatively, you could have used the .NOT. operator to simplify the command sequence even more. For example:

```
store 0 to ind
if .not. (year=curyr .or. year=lastyr)
  store 1 to ind
endif
if .not. (month > 0 .and. month < 13)
  store 1 to ind
endif
if .not. (day > 0 .and. day < 32)
```

```
      store 1 to ind
   endif
   if ind=0
      do label
      return
   else
      @ 9,1 say "Invalid Date"
   endif
enddo
```

Remember that when the DATE() function is used, you have to see to it that the correct date is supplied to dBase II when it loads or that the SET DATE TO command forms part of your command file.

There are many ways of validating dates and some users will want to go further and check that the day is valid in respect of the month (e.g. reject 30 February). Other users will want to write the most concise possible date checking routine. We are now going to leave the Name and Address Labels program behind and concentrate on building a routine that is less long-winded than the earlier examples. Subsequently we will improve it so that it also checks for the correct number of days in the month, even to the extent of ensuring that the 29th February is valid in a leap year. The method consists of using a DO loop that will continue until the date is valid:

```
set talk off
store 0 to month,day
store "      " to datex
do while  month < 1 .or. month > 12;
   .or.  day < 1   .or. day > 31
   erase
   if .not. (day=0.and.month=0)
      @ 9,1 say "Invalid Date"
   endif
   @ 5,1  say "Enter Date in form YYMMDD" get datex picture "999999"
   read
   store val($(datex,5,2)) to day
   store val($(datex,3,2)) to month
   store val($(datex,1,2)) to year
enddo
erase
```

On the first time through the routine, the DO WHILE test will find an invalid day and month because it will be comparing against the zeroised memory variables. The program will thus continue to execute and ask the user to enter a date. The substring function ($) is used to extract the day, month, and year respectively, while the VAL function converts them to numeric variables. Control then returns to the DO command which contains the validation tests. If none of the tests are true, i.e. if the month is not less than 1 or greater than 12 and the day is not less than 1 or greater than 31, the DO loop will end and the program will resume at the command following the ENDDO command. If any of the tests are true, i.e. if the date is false, the loop will continue so that the user will again be asked for the date. Meanwhile, another first time through condition will fail – that of zero day and month variables – so that the Invalid Date message will be displayed. The routine will thus simply loop around until a valid date is supplied. Let us add a check on the correct number of days in the month.

```
set talk off
store 0 to month,day,topday
store "       " to datex
do while    month < 1      .or. month > 12;
     .or.   day < 1        .or. day > topday
   erase
   if .not. (day=0.and.month=0)
     @ 9,1 say "Invalid Date"
   endif
   @ 5,1 say "Enter Date in form YYMMDD" get datex picture "999999"
   read
   store val($(datex,5,2)) to day
   store val($(datex,3,2)) to month
   store val($(datex,1,2)) to year
   store str(int(29-(year/4.0 -int(year/4.0))),2) to feb
   store val($("31"+feb+"31303130313130313031",month*2-1,2)) to topday
enddo
erase
```

Instead of comparing the day against 31, we are comparing it against the contents of the variable Topday. We will thus need to store into Topday the highest day: the month supplied by the user. A simple way of doing this is to use the month number as part of the substring function ($) and extract the highest day from a table which is set up to contain 31 for month 01, 28 for month 02, 31 for month 03, etc.:

$("312831303130313130313031",month*2-1,2)

Thus, March will result in position 3*2–1, i.e. 5, and the characters 31 will be extracted. The VAL function will convert the character variable to a numeric variable. If it were not for leap years, that would be the end of it. Unfortunately, we have to test against 29 not 28 if the year is divisible by 4. Let us try the following:

int(29-(year/4.0 -int(year/4.0)))

If we divide the year by 4.0 it will give a result which contains a fraction when the year is not a multiple of 4. However, the same division by 4 using the integer function will give a result which is a whole number, i.e. without the fraction. If we subtract the second result from the first result, we will be left with only the fraction. Had the year been a multiple of 4 there would not, of course, have been a fraction. So, if the fraction is zero, the year is a leap year and has 29 days in February. All we have to do now is to subtract the fraction from 29 and obtain the integer result. If we subtract a zero function, it will result in 29; otherwise the result will be 28. Next we use the STR function to convert the arithmetic result into characters and store it into a variable called Feb.

```
store str(int(29-(year/4.0 -int(year/4.0))),2) to feb
```

Finally, we introduce the variable Feb into our table of highest days in place of the "28" we had originally:

```
store val($("31"+feb+"3130313031313031",month*2-1,2)) to topday
```

Incidentally, if the user supplies an invalid month, e.g. 13, the dBase II message "Beyond String" will appear as a consequence of the program trying to use a position on the table which is beyond the end of the table. However, the user will never see the message because the ERASE command which comes next clears the screen too quickly.

Chapter Ten
Functions and Techniques

Functions

A function is simply another operator, much the same as + or −, which performs a set task. The function EOF, for example, tests for the end of the file and provides you with a simple means of telling whether you have reached that condition or not.

Certain functions have already been described, but for the sake of presenting all the functions together they will be covered again. Rather than deal with the functions alphabetically or in some other equally unhelpful sequence, we are going to group them as follows:

(1) Those related to files and records:

     #   : current record number
     *   : deleted record indicator
     EOF   : end of file indicator
     FILE : file existence indicator

(2) Those related to numeric or character fields:

     INT   : to discard the fraction and return only the integer value
     $: to obtain a character field which is part of another character field
     STR   : to turn a numeric field into a character field
     VAL   : to turn a character field into a numeric field
     TRIM : to display or print a character field without allowing trailing blanks to take up space
     LEN   : to find out how many characters a character field contains
     @   : to find out whether and where a character field is contained in another character field
     !   : to convert lower-case characters to upper-case

Functions and Techniques **129**

(3) Miscellaneous functions.

- DATE ( ) : to obtain the date from the dBase II stored date
- RANK : applies to a single character and obtains the value of the character, e.g. its sort sequence in relation to other characters
- CHR : produces a character which represents a given numeric value
- TYPE : indicates the type, i.e. character, numeric, or logical, of a field

Files and records

#

The # function has been used several times in illustrations earlier in this book. It provides the current record number and is particularly useful as a means of checking on the result of a FIND command, which either returns the record number of the required record when the FIND was successful, or a zero record number otherwise.

f
#

*

The asterisk has already been observed in signalling a deleted record, e.g. when the LIST command has been used. It may also be used as a function in the same context. By testing it, you are able to determine whether or not a record has been deleted. For example:

f
*

```
if  *
    skip
else
    @ lines, 10 say title
    skip
```

The asterisk function returns a true or false condition depending on whether or not the current record has been marked for deletion.

EOF

This function is most often used in command files as part of the DO WHILE command to control the execution of subsequent commands. It allows you to specify a sequence of actions in respect of each record as it is read, until the last record has participated in the sequence. At that point it signals the end of the DO WHILE sequence.

f
EOF

FILE

The FILE function is very useful in a command file when you want to test that a file you are about to use is actually present, i.e. that the

f
FILE

diskette containing the file has been loaded. The function operates on a True/False principle. For example:

    if file ("books")

will yield a True value if the file is present. The filename may be given as an actual filename between quote marks or as a temporary field without the quote marks. The following is identical in effect to the example above:

    store "books" to filename
    if file(filename)

INT

The integer function provides a means of discarding the decimal part of a value, i.e. the fraction, to return the integer or whole number. The whole number will retain its sign, i.e. it will remain negative if the value was negative to start with. You may round up by adding .5 to the value. For example, if the cost is 19.60, int (cost + 0.5) will give 20, but int (cost) will give 19.

$

The substring function selects part of a character field according to the parameters, which are:

    fieldname
    start position
    number of characters

Examples are:

    . store $("James",1,1) to init
    J
    . store $("James",1,2) to init
    Ja
    . store $("James",2,4) to init
    ames

STR

There are some operations which are possible only on character fields, e.g. the substring function. The STR function will convert a numeric field to character format to take advantage of these facilities. The parameters of the STR function are as follows:

```
fieldname
length of character field
number of decimals to be included
```

The specified length must provide a field long enough to contain all the digits (including the decimal point if decimals are required). The STR function is prepared to discard decimals if you specify none, but insists on a field long enough to contain all the integers.

The following examples show how the parameters affect the conversion of a numeric field COST which contains 19.65.

```
. store str(cost,2,0) to costchar
19

. store str(cost,2,2) to costchar
**

. store str(cost,5,2) to costchar
19.65

. store str(cost,7,2) to costchar
  19.65

. store str(cost,7,3) to costchar
 19.650

. store str(cost,5,0) to costchar
   19

. store str(cost,1,0) to costchar
*
```

A result of asterisks indicates that the function has been used with illegal parameters. It is possible to specify a numeric value or an expression, e.g. 201*.5/400, in place of the fieldname. Although the third parameter has been shown in all cases, you do not need to include it if no decimals are required. The substring function is often used when printing numeric variables. For example:

```
@ 1,1 say "Page "+str(pageno,3)
```

VAL

This function is the converse of STR in that it converts a character field which contains leading numerics (including a decimal point and its sign if required) to a numeric field. Only the integer part of the value in the character field will be transferred to the numeric field. For example:

```
. store "19.65" to costchar
19.65
. store val(costchar) to cost
19

. store "-56.898" to char2
-56.898
. store val(char2) to cost2
-56

. store val(88.342) to cost3
88
```

The substring function may be used within the parentheses.

TRIM

This function removes trailing spaces in a character field. It is most useful when printing or displaying data. For example:

```
. display inits,name
D.H.      Ford

. display trim(inits)," ",name
D.H. Ford
```

LEN

The length function only applies to character fields. It provides the length of a character field. Beware though; spaces or blanks are also considered to be characters. If you want to ignore trailing spaces, you should include the TRIM function. For example:

```
. ? len("abcdef     ")
11

. store title to titlex
As You Like It
. ? len(titlex)
40

. ? len(trim(titlex))
14
```

@
This is the substring search function. It searches a character field for a specified character or set of characters. For example:

```
. ? @("Chess",title)
12
```

The above will tell you that the word Chess is contained in the Title field (which in this example contains "Beginner's Chess") at position 12, i.e. starting at the twelfth character. If the specified character(s) had not been found, a value of 0 would have been returned. In a command file you could use it as a condition:

```
if @("Chess",title) = 0
     skip
else
     @ lines,5 say title
     @ lines,50 say supplier
```

!
This function converts lower-case to upper-case. It is useful when you want to search for an item regardless of case. If we repeat our substring search from the previous function, it could be more successful this way:

```
store !(title) to titlecase
if @("CHESS",titlecase)=0
     skip
else
     @ lines,5 say title
     @ lines,50 say supplier
```

The above will list titles which contain the word "Chess" or "chess" or even "CHess".

Miscellaneous functions
DATE ()
This function returns an eight-character field in the form MM/DD/YY, e.g. 09/25/84. The date is taken from the stored dBase II date which is either supplied by you or, in the case of MS-DOS (PC-DOS), taken from the DOS system date, when you load the program. It may also have been set with the SET DATE TO command. The function may be used to display the date or STORE the date. For example:

```
@ 1,1 say date()
```

or

    store date( ) to datestor

The parentheses never contain anything. They are there only to tell dBase II that it is a function, not a field called Date.

RANK
This function (available in version 2.4) provides you with a means of obtaining the value of a character to see where the character ranks in relation to other characters. For example, on the IBM PC, RANK("A") will produce 65 while RANK("B") will produce 66. The name of a field may be supplied in place of the character itself, but only the left-most character of the field will be evaluated. For example:

    rank (author)

will return 65 if the field Author contains "Austen, Jane".

CHR
This is the opposite to RANK in that the function CHR will convert a numeric value to the equivalent character. For example, CHR(65) will produce the character A. You may specify a fieldname in place of the numeric value. For example:

    . store 65 to number
       65
    . ? chr(number)
    A

TYPE
The TYPE function returns a C, N, or L depending on the field. For example:

    . store 65 to number
       65
    . ? type(number)
    N

    . store F to indicator
    .F.
    . ? type(indicator)
    L

    . ? type("Dickens")
    C

SET commands

There are 26 SET commands, 19 of them of the on/off variety, e.g. SET TALK OFF, and 7 of the SET TO variety, e.g. SET DATE TO. We are going to ignore the distinction and deal with them in alphabetic sequence because it will be easier afterwards to look up a particular SET command if they are listed alphabetically.

• SET ALTERNATE TO is used to specify the name of a disk file to which everything that normally appears on the screen will be written. This includes the user input as well as dBase II output but does not include the results of @ SAY commands. The file will have a .TXT suffix and will be created if it does not already exist. Output to the file may be switched on and off with the SET ALTERNATE ON/OFF command. Details written to the .TXT file may subsequently be included in a word processing document.

• SET ALTERNATE is used to switch on or off the facility of writing dBase II output and user input to a specified .TXT file. It requires a SET ALTERNATE TO command to have been issued previously. Default is OFF.

• SET BELL is used to turn the alarm bell, e.g. at end of field, on or off. When the bell is on you are notified by the bell (a beep, really) when you have reached the end of a field (e.g. in full-screen APPEND or EDIT mode) and dBase II automatically switches to the next field. Touch-typists find it useful because they are often not looking at the screen. Others find the constant noise irritating and switch it off. See also the SET CONFIRM command. The bell is also used when you have used format characters in a PICTURE field with the @ GET command and the user attempts to enter an illegal character, such as an alphabetic character into a PICTURE "9999" field. Default is ON.

• SET CARRY has been covered in some detail in Chapter 2. SET CARRY ON is used when in the APPEND mode to display details from the previous record entered and is useful in saving you the work of re-entering details which are the same from one record to the next. You may use the return key or CTRL and X to move past such fields without changing their contents. Default is OFF.

• SET COLON OFF may be used to avoid displaying the field boundaries (i.e. the colons) when you use the @ GET command. Default is ON.

• SET CONFIRM ON may be used when in full-screen APPEND or EDIT mode to prevent dBase II from automatically skipping to the next field when the end of the current field has been reached. If you keep typing, the final character will change continuously to reflect what you are entering but the cursor will not move on to the next field until you have pressed the return key or used CTRL and X. If the bell is on (see SET BELL) a beep will sound for every character you attempt to enter past the end of the field. Default is OFF.

● SET CONSOLE is used to turn the screen on or off as an output device. It can be useful if you want a user to enter a password but do not want to have it appear on the screen. When you issue the SET CONSOLE OFF command from the keyboard you may be disconcerted by the sudden absence of the next dot prompt. However, you may continue to enter commands (albeit blindly) and they will be executed but you will not see anything on the screen until after you have issued the SET CONSOLE ON command. Default is ON.

● SET DATE TO is used to set or change the date.

● SET DEBUG ON is a specialised SET PRINT ON command and is used when you are trying to iron out the errors (or bugs) in a command file. You will already be using SET ECHO ON and possibly SET STEP ON, but will want to have the results of those two SET commands displayed on the printer so that they do not clutter up the screen. Default is OFF.

● SET DEFAULT TO has been described in Chapter 3. It specifies the drive on which dBase II expects to find files.

● SET DELETED is used to control the execution of certain commands such as COUNT, LIST, FIND, etc., in respect of records marked for deletion. If, for example, you have issued the SET DELETED ON command, COUNT will not include any records marked for deletion. Default is OFF, i.e. all commands other than COPY, APPEND FROM and SUM will treat a record carrying a deleted marker like any other. Default is OFF.

● SET ECHO ON is used to display command file lines as they are executed to assist you in following the results of the command file. You may direct this output to the printer with the SET DEBUG ON command. Default is OFF.

● SET EJECT is used with the REPORT command to control the ejection to a new page (ON) before starting the report, or starting the report immediately (OFF). Default is ON.

● SET ESCAPE ON permits you to cancel the execution of a command file by pressing the escape key, whereas the OFF condition will prevent such an escape. Default is ON.

● SET EXACT ON is used with the FIND command to specify that an exact match must be made, i.e. the characters following that given in the FIND command may only be trailing spaces. This SET command may similarly specify that an expression provides a full match and not just a match on the characters given in the second part of an equation. For example, IF AUTHOR = "Dick" should not accept Dickens. Default is OFF.

- SET FORMAT TO has been discussed in Chapter 8. It is used to direct output of @ SAY commands either to the screen or the printer by issuing a SET FORMAT TO SCREEN or SET FORMAT TO PRINT command respectively. It may also be used to obtain @ commands from a format file (.FMT) on disk.
- SET HEADING TO may be used to specify an additional page heading to be printed with the output from the REPORT command. No quotation delimiter marks are required. See Chapter 3.
- SET INDEX TO is used to set an alternative index or indexes. The specified index(es) will replace those currently in use.
- SET INTENSITY controls the use of inverse video or dual intensity on the screen during the operation of commands like APPEND, MODIFY COMMAND, etc. Default is ON.
- SET LINKAGE ON is used with SELECT SECONDARY and SELECT PRIMARY as a means of linking movement on the two files, so that a command which performs a scope operation, such as SUM WHILE, will move the current record pointer on in both files in keeping with the condition supplied in the command. Default is OFF.
- SET MARGIN TO provides a user control over the positioning of a report. All print lines will be moved to the right by the number of positions specified.
- SET PRINT ON directs dBase II output to the printer. It does not include the output from @ commands for which you have to issue the SET FORMAT TO PRINT command as well. Default is OFF.
- SET RAW ON will stop the single spaces which appear between fields when you use the LIST or DISPLAY command. Default is OFF.
- SET SCREEN OFF will prevent the full-screen operation of commands like APPEND, EDIT, etc. In APPEND mode, for example, you will be asked for the details one field at a time. If you exceed a given field length, the program will ask you to re-enter the field. Default is ON.
- SET STEP ON is used to single-step your way through a command file. After each command, you will be asked if you want to do another step (i.e. another single command) or cancel the command

138 *Working With dBase II*

file, or enter a command from the keyboard. If SET ECHO ON had also been issued, each command will be displayed prior to the selection message. Default is OFF.
• SET TALK OFF is used in command files to prevent the display of dBase II messages such as the current record number, etc. Default is ON.

Version 2.4 of dBase II contains a new command, the DISPLAY STATUS command. It shows the current condition of all the on/off SET commands except for SET SCREEN. (It is a curious omission since SET CONSOLE is included.) However, you will find the DISPLAY STATUS command very useful when you have changed some of the default settings and need to review your position.

Special techniques

This section has not been provided to supply you with a complete guide to extra techniques, but simply to whet your appetite. dBase II has a powerful language and you will, no doubt, find your own way of putting it to good use. The examples below are there merely to introduce you to the possibilities which are open to you.

Initialising character memory variables
When you want to use a memory variable in an @ GET command, it will be necessary to initialise the memory variable first, usually with the STORE command. For example:

```
store "                                        " to authorx
```

This is a clumsy method which involves counting the number of spaces between the quote marks if you want to get the number of characters exactly right. An alternative and more attractive method relies on using the STR and $ functions. First you set up a large character field containing spaces, the length determined by the largest memory variable you will want to use in an @ GET command. If we assume a 40-character maximum, we set the character field up as follows:

```
store str(1,41) to spaces
```

The STR function will create a character field 41 characters long containing the decimal value 1. The latter will be in position 41 of the character field and the preceding 40 positions will be set to spaces. We now have a character field containing 40 spaces from which we may select as many as we need on each occasion by using the $ function. For example:

    store $(spaces,1,25) to authorx

    store $(spaces,1,2) to supcodex

    store $(spaces,1,15) to classx

Note that this method limits you to 128 characters. If you try a larger number, the memory variable will be created but it will contain asterisks.

Load and go
You can execute a command file as part of loading dBase II by providing the filename of the command file as part of the load instruction:

    dbase bookenq

dBase II will be loaded and the operating system will pass to it any parameters which formed part of the load instruction. dBase II is geared to see such a parameter as the name of a command file and will issue an internal DO to execute the command file.

Formatting APPEND and EDIT screens
If you are using APPEND, EDIT, etc., in full-screen mode, you may format your own screen by creating a .FMT file containing the necessary @ SAY GET commands and issuing the SET FORMAT TO command prior to issuing the APPEND or EDIT command. If say the .FMT file was BOOKS.FMT, you would enter the following:

    . set format to books
    . append

Remember afterwards to cancel the SET command by issuing a SET FORMAT TO SCREEN command.

Variable GO TO
If you want to use the GO command in a command file to position the current record pointer to a specific record, you can use a memory variable as part of the GO command. The contents of the memory variable will specify the record number. For example:

```
input "How many records do you want to go back?" to back
store #-back to back
if back > 0
```

```
     go back
else
  ? "You cannot go back that far. Current record is ",#
```

Multiple field FIND
If you have to do a FIND on an indexed item that includes embedded spaces, such as two fields with trailing spaces after the first field, the FIND command will ignore the second field unless you surround both fields with quotes. For example:

```
. use books index locauth
. find "Hall    Dickens"
```

Duplicate records
Files that contain duplicate records may be cleaned up with the TOTAL command. The latter will write a record on every change of a specified field, so if you specify the field which identifies the duplication, TOTAL will write out every record except those that are duplicates of a preceding record. The file must be indexed or sorted on that field. Unfortunately, you cannot specify more than one field so this method is effective only where the file has a key field such as Custcode on our Customer file.

WAIT TO
The WAIT command can be used to store a user response into a memory variable. For example:

```
wait to reply
if reply = "N"
```

WAIT TO provides an additional run-time control over the execution of the command file.

Validation of screen input
The CLEAR GETS command may be used to great effect when you are validating screen input and need to go back to the user on an invalid item. Let us assume that you have a screenful of @ GET fields that have been READ and you are validating each one in turn. When you reach the fourth field you discover that it is invalid. You do not want to ask the user to re-enter all the fields, nor do you want to clear the screen and have him lose sight of what has already been entered. Ideally, you want to reposition the cursor at the invalid field on a screen which still contains everything previously entered. At the bottom of the screen there would be a message indicating that the

field in question was invalid. This time you want the READ command to return only the one field.

All of the above may be done very simply:

(1) Issue the CLEAR GETS command.
(2) Reissue the @ GET command for the error field only, using the same screen coordinates as before.
(3) Display an appropriate error message.
(4) Follow that with a READ (which will transfer just the one field) and revalidation.

Passwords

If you want to restrict user access to certain command files by checking for an appropriate password, you could include the following simple routine in your command file:

```
set talk off
store F to pass
do while .not. pass
  ? "Enter Password"
  set console off
  accept to password
  set console on
  if password="SECRET"
    store T to pass
  endif
enddo
```

The SET CONSOLE OFF command will prevent the password from displaying on the screen as the user is entering it. If the user is canny enough to list the command file, the password will be discovered but see Chapter 11 for details of dBase II RunTime.

Substring validation

When you need to test that a user response is one of several set replies, such as Y,y,X,x, etc., try using a DO loop together with the substring function. For example:

```
store " " to reply
do while .not. reply$"YyXx"
   accept "Please Select One of the Above" to reply
enddo
```

The DO loop will trap the user until he has provided an acceptable reply. The substring function will test whether the contents of the variable reply is contained in the string of acceptable replies. The substring function is equally valuable in other situations when you need to test for one of a number of possible and acceptable conditions. For example:

```
if month$"JANFEBMARAPRMAYJUNJULAUGSEPOCTNOVDEC"
```

Macro substitution within a string
You may introduce the contents of a variable into a character string, such as a print heading, without treating the variable as a separate field. For example:

```
@ 1,30 say "LIST OF BOOKS BY &author   CLASSIFICATION &class"
```

More than 32 fields
dBase II limits you to 32 fields per record but you can get around this restriction by using two or more records to contain the information. What you need to do is to provide a Record Type field which contains, say, "A" for the first type of record, "B" for the second, and so on. There should also be a key field, such as Customer Code, which may be used to tie the two records together. The fields for Record Type "B" will be identical to those for Record Type "A", but they will contain different information. It will be up to you to document the differences and to remember to use the fields correctly.

Data economy
If you need to store data with a lot of redundant characters, such as names and addresses, and you cannot afford the wasted space resulting from the use of fixed length fields, try using the TRIM function to store the details as a continuous stream of characters with separator characters between fields. For example:

```
Anderson,Mr.,K.R.,22 Dolphin Square,Front Street,Middle Town
```

You would still need to define a dBASE II field to contain the stream of characters, so you would need to decide beforehand how many characters you are going to allow as a maximum. Let us say that after investigation, we concluded that the majority of names and addresses would fit into 75 characters. Those that could not, would be abbreviated by the user. Thus, Square would become Sq.

There are two important points to consider:

(1) The separator character. Choose a character that sorts lower than any alphabetic character so that, for example, "Anders" would precede "Anderson" if you were to index the field.

(2) Although you are obtaining a great deal of benefit at the computer end by storing several fields as one, there is no need to inflict this presentation on the user. You should continue to present the user with fields which are convenient to him or her, both on data entry and data display. This will involve you in joining user-supplied fields together with the TRIM function before storing the data, and in using the substring ($) and substring search (@) functions to explode the composite field into its constituent parts before displaying it. Let us look at one technique for unscrambling a composite field containing comma separators. The composite field is called Nameaddr and its user-friendly version looks like this:

    Surname
    Initials
    Title, eg. Mr
    Address Line 1
    Address Line 2
    Address Line 3
    Address Line 4

The 7 fields which will contain the above have fieldnames consisting of Name1, Name2, Name3, etc.:

```
store 1 to counter
store 1 to start
do while counter < 8 .and. start < 76
   store $(nameaddr,start,76-start)+"," to part
   store "name"+str(counter,1) to field
*
   store @(",",part) to nochars
   store $(nameaddr,start,nochars-1) to &field
*
   store start + nochars to start
   store counter + 1 to counter
enddo
```

Documentation

Computer programmers traditionally dislike the task of documenting what they are doing, but all would agree that the documentation of any application is essential. You should ideally maintain a folder containing the following for each application:

- A brief description of the application.

- A note on the databases and indexes used for the application.
- The structure of each database.
- The contents of all the command and format files.
- A list of the memory variables used by each command file.
- A chart showing the inter-relationship of the command files.
- Details of any report files.
- A user guide which explains to the user how to start, how to escape from a screen, what conventions have been laid down for data entry, etc.

It might seem like a lot but you will find it well worth the trouble when afterwards you come to make changes. Remember to date the documentation both at the start and when you make changes. The user guide should, of course, be reproduced and issued to each user.

It is a good idea to provide descriptive lines within the command files and format files. The NOTE or * command may be used not only to explain the purpose of the complete file, but also to explain parts of the program. You could, moreover, add an explanatory comment to certain command lines. For example, you could explain the purpose of an IF command on the ENDIF line:

```
if titlex = "    "
   erase
   return
endif    *Test if user has asked to exit
```

Another form of documentation is the use of the REMARK command which will also display the comment. For example:

```
remark Title Enquiry
remark You may leave the screen by pressing Return
```

Since a large part of the reason for having good documentation lies in providing a clear presentation of the application, we should also include in this discussion the subject of coding, that is, the methods used in writing programs. The following rules should be followed:

(1) Use indentation to show clearly the commands that are part of a DO loop or an IF command sequence.

(2) If you are designing an application that uses fields from more than one database, consider giving the fieldnames an identifying prefix so that the file origin of a field is immediately clear. In our illustrations, we could have prefixed all fields from the BOOKS file with B:, all fields from the supplier file with S:, and all files from the

Customer file with C:. For example:

```
b:title
s:name
c:surname
```

(3) There is a frequently used approach to using upper- and lower-case in command files which consists of showing all dBase II keywords in upper-case and all fieldnames and memory variables in lower-case. This can make it easier to follow a command file. The author pleads guilty to not using that approach in this book for the very good reason that the latter had different objectives. Consideration was given to the needs of mixing text and dBASE II language, rather than to documentation requirements. You, however, are concerned with presenting your command file logic in a purely dBASE II environment and you may find the approach a very useful one.

An easy way of tying together the various command and format files for documentation purposes is to use a word processing package and merge the contents of the files into a document (see Appendix B). This has the advantage that no transcription errors will occur during the preparation of the documentation.

Chapter Eleven
Linking With Other Programs

External files

The data in a dBase II database file cannot readily be accessed by other programs such as a word processor, or spreadsheet, or even a programming language like BASIC or COBOL. There is, however, a method of copying some or all of a database to an external file which will be in standard ASCII format and thus accessible to other programs. The COPY command together with the SDF clause is used to create such an external file. All the usual COPY command keywords such as FOR, WHILE, etc., are available, but the SDF keyword must be included. For example:

```
. use books
. copy to book for author="Dickens" sdf
```

The file will be created as BOOK.TXT. You may specify the full filename if you prefer a different suffix. Each record on this file will be as long as the database record itself, not counting the extra character used by dBase II. The details will appear much as they would if you were to show them with the LIST command but without a record number or separating spaces between fields. The problem with this format is that an external program would not know where a field started or ended since it would see the record simply as a long string of characters. This may be overcome by adding the word DELIMITED to the command. For example:

```
. copy to book sdf delimited
```

This time the fields will be separated by commas and the alphabetic fields enclosed in quote marks. You may specify a different delimiting character by including the latter in the command. To separate fields not by commas but by, say, oblique strokes, you would add WITH /. For example:

. copy to book sdf delimited with /

So far, each field has been written to the external file exactly as it appears in the database. If you do not want any trailing spaces or leading zeros, you specify a comma as the delimiting character as, for instance:

. copy to book sdf delimited with ,

The fields will no longer be enclosed in quotes and empty fields will be indicated only by the presence of the commas which would have followed them had they contained data. This is how it would look:

```
As You Like It,Shakespeare,Drama,3,5.48,,BW,4,0.99
Pride and Prejudice,Austen,Jane,Novel,3,9.00,c,MA,4,8.00
Dombey and Son,Dickens,Novel,2,4.75,a,BW,2,2.50
Treasure Island,Stevenson,R L,Novel,1,4.00,,BW,1,3.99
Turn of the Screw,James,Henry,Novel,0,0.00,a,d,CA,2,9.00
Far from the Madding Crowd,Hardy,Thomas,Novel,4,8.99,,CA,6,3.00
Islands of Greece,The,Jones,T B,Travel,1,0.00,a,CA,1,1.11
Microwave Cookery,Jones,Belinda,Cooking,0,0.00,d,MA,1,2.50
Indian Dishes,Anderson,K L,Cooking,1,4.00,,MA,2,2.00
Kings and Queens of England,Delderfield,R F,History,5,12.50,b,CA,6,9.00
Crime and Punishment,Dostoievsky,Novel,0,0.00,b,CA,1,3.50
,,,0,0,,,0,0
```

You may also append data from an external file by using the SDF clause with the APPEND FROM command. dBase II expects the fields on the external file to be delimited by commas. It will strip quotes and commas and load the data into the dBase II file then in USE. There are two forms:

. append from extfile sdf

or

. append from extfile sdf delimited

The command does not allow you to specify a delimiting character since only commas are accepted but you must include the word DELIMITED if the fields are separated. If, for example, you had created an external file with COPY SDF DELIMITED and then tried to APPEND SDF without specifying the DELIMITED keyword, dBase II would fill each field with as many characters as it required including the separating commas and any quotes surrounding alphabetic fields. Packages which provide the means of creating delimited files include 1-2-3 and Supercalc.

While we are thinking in terms of using the COPY command to create delimited files for spreadsheet programs such as 1-2-3 or

Supercalc, or the Mailmerge facilities of Wordstar, and non-delimited files for other word processing purposes, let us not forget that the SET ALTERNATE commands also provide the means of writing to an external file. You could, for example, output the contents of a database with commands such as LIST, REPORT, ?, COUNT and SUM. For example:

```
. set alternate to extfile
. set alternate on
. use books
. sum cost,nobought
 66.29    42
. list author,trim(title) off
. set alternate off
```

The external file would be called EXTFILE.TXT and would contain all the user input and dBase II output between the SET ALTERNATE ON and SET ALTERNATE OFF commands:

```
. use books
. sum cost,nobought
 66.29    42
. list author,trim(title) off
Shakespeare            As You Like It
Austen,Jane            Pride and Prejudice
Dickens                Dombey and Son
Stevenson,R L          Treasure Island
James,Henry            Turn of the Screw
Hardy,Thomas           Far from the Madding Crowd
Jones,T B              Islands of Greece,The
Hall,F J               Devon and Cornwall
Jones,Belinda          Microwave Cookery
Anderson,K L           Indian Dishes
Delderfield,R F        Kings and Queens of England
Finberg,H P R          Formation of England,The
Shakespeare            Henry V
Chaucer                Canterbury Tales
Tolstoy                War and Peace
```

Command generators and utilities

There are at least eight software packages which have come along in the wake of dBase II and are either based on dBase II files, or aimed at generating dBase II command files to save programming effort.

The code generators are as follows: Zip; Quickcode; and Autocode. The other packages are: dUtil; DBPlus; dGraph; Abstat; and RunTime.

Zip
Zip generates dBase II code specifically for formatting input screens and printed reports. It is essentially an @ SAY GET generator which allows you to use the screen to paint the data entry screen or the printed output. It also lets you add your own dBase II commands which will be merged with the generated @ commands. This is less of an option than an essential since the commands you would add include commands such as USE, DO WHILE, etc. Zip creates .FMT files and .CMD or .PRG files. It also stores the screen you painted so that you can change details without starting from scratch.

Quickcode
This Fox & Geller product generates both the database (i.e. it performs a function equivalent to the CREATE command) and a set of program files which perform various functions such as producing reports or finding records.

When you load the program, it provides you with a menu from which you select the various options. Your first selection will be the Quickscreen option which presents you with a blank screen and allows you to set it up as you want to see it for data entry purposes. You may provide as much descriptive detail as you wish but you are essentially defining the contents of the database. The fieldnames for the database are also entered on the screen, prefixed by semicolons to identify them as such. You may then enter the Fields mode which will present you with your defined fields and give you the option of changing the allocated length or field type as well as specifying minimum and maximum values, etc., for validation purposes. When you have completed your revisions, Quickcode generates the database and a set of programs which perform functions which are the equivalent of the APPEND, EDIT, INDEX, FIND, REPORT, etc. There are also programs which perform validation, create mailing labels, and create Wordstar data files. Twelve programs in all are generated.

Autocode
This program by Stemmos Ltd. requires you to set up a file describing the screen (you may use a word processor or Autocode's own Editor), and then proceed through a series of code generation

steps which operate in a question-and-answer mode to create a menu, file maintenance routines, and reports. To run the code, you call up the command file which contains the menu and that, in turn, will take you to the other options.

dUtil

dUtil provides a set of utilities for merging command files, converting command file grammar to the standard of upper-case for dBase II keywords and indented lines between IF and ENDIF pairs, etc. The method of merging related command files (e.g. a menu and the command files called by the menu) consists of replacing DO command file commands with the actual command files themselves. The theory is that it will require less disk accesses, and hence execute faster, if all the commands are in memory at the same time. dUtil is a Fox & Geller product.

DBPlus

This program by Humansoft offers three services:

(1) It has a fast and flexible sort. The sort is claimed to be 15 times faster than the dBase II SORT command, and 3 times faster then the INDEX command. It also allows you to sort on more than one field at a time.

(2) It provides a means of compressing databases to between 30% and 40% of the original size for back-up purposes. The database cannot be used in compressed form by dBase II, so you have to decompress it if you want to use it.

(3) A transform utility which provides a simple and powerful equivalent to the MODIFY STRUCTURE command, or which will create Wordstar compatible files from the database contents.

dGraph

The graph-drawing package is another Fox & Geller product. It will read a dBase II database file and draw one of four graphs based on the data in the file: bar chart or histogram, line graph, pie chart, and a cross between a bar chart and a pie chart called a piebar chart.

If you visualise the data as rows represented by records and columns represented by fields, dGraph will allow you a maximum of 52 rows and 4 columns for any one graph. This means, for example, that you can have up to four different lines on a line graph.

Abstat

This is a statistics and graphics program that will operate on numeric fields in dBase II database files. Two kinds of graph may be produced: bar charts or histograms, and scatter graphs. Nearly 20 statistical commands are provided including linear regression, correlation coefficients, standard deviation, Chi square, etc. Abstat also allows you to format reports, write to dBase II files, read or write ASCII files, and sort data. It is an Anderson-Bell product.

RunTime

RunTime is a product by Ashton-Tate who, of course, produced dBase II itself. It consists of two programs. dBCode compresses dBase II command files so that they cannot be listed in intelligible form or modified. A second program, dBRun, will execute the compressed code without requiring dBase II itself to be present.

This means that applications written in dBase II can be sold or distributed without incurring the cost of dBase II each time, and without fear of users tampering with the code or having the design and internal working of the application pirated. RunTime licences are available direct from Ashton-Tate.

Appendix A
dBase II Program Files

It will help you to know something about the files which contain the dBase II software, particularly in situations where a large application forces you to try and find every scrap of space you can on a diskette. The dBase II version 2.3 program resides in 12 files:

DBASE.COM	Main program
DBASEMSG.COM	Messages
DBASEMAI.OVR	Main overlay
DBASEMSC.OVR	Miscellaneous
DBASEAPP.OVR	Append
DBASEBRO.OVR	Browse
DBASEJOI.OVR	Join
DBASEMOD.OVR	Modify
DBASERPG.OVR	Report form
DBASESRT.OVR	Sort
DBASETTL.OVR	Total
DBASEUPD.OVR	Update

As you can see from the descriptions above, many of the files represent individual dBase II commands. Unless you require these functions, you may remove all but the first five files to give yourself more space on the diskette which contains the dBase II program.

Similarly, version 2.4 has the following:

DBASE.COM
DBASEOVR.COM
DBASEMSG.TXT

The final file contains extensive HELP messages but may be removed if you do not intend to invoke the HELP facilities.

Appendix B
Word Processing and dBase II

As we have seen already, dBase II provides an interface with word processors in the sense of transferring information from a database to an external file which may be processed by a word processing package. There is, however, another link with word processors: several of the standard dBase II files may be set up or modified using any standard word processing package. These include REPORT files (.FRM), command files (.CMD or .PRG) and format files (.FMT). On top of that, you may want to include a document created by a word processor in a dBase II command file to take advantage of the TEXT command which made its appearance in version 2.4. Let us look at these facilities in more detail.

Many users of dBase II use a word processor to create their Command and Format files. One reason is that the dBase II editor is too limiting in what it displays, restricts you in moving about on the screen, and does not allow you to copy commands to another part of the command file. Just about any word processing package will save you time when you start creating your programs. Any dBase II command that is repetitive, particularly the @SAY or @ SAY GET statements, may be copied as many times as you need it. All you have to do then is to use the word processing edit keys to change the copied sections, which is a lot quicker than having to type in every command individually.

One of the best known word processing packages, Wordstar, has a means of executing an external program, such as dBase II, without having to return to the operating system. When you QUIT dBase II, you return to Wordstar. This allows you to set up a command file with a word processor, go into dBase II to try it out, and return to the word processor to correct it. (If you have Wordstar and dBase II on separate diskettes and you cannot get the transfer to work, try setting the logged drive to the one that contains dBase II.) Another attraction of Wordstar is that it uses the same cursor control keys as dBase II. It is recommended that you use the non-document mode of Wordstar when you create dBase II command or format files.

You can also copy a word processing document into your command file. Again using Wordstar as an example, this consists simply of opening your command file as a word processing document (in non-document mode) and using the Wordstar CTRL and KR commands to copy in the text which you had previously set up as a word processing file.

Finally you will find it useful, if you are using a word processing package to do your documentation, to copy your command files and format files directly into your documentation files.

Appendix C
Summary of dBase II Commands

This summary of dBase II commands has been reproduced by kind permission of Ashton-Tate (UK) Ltd.

CONVENTIONS
TYPOGRAPHICAL CONVENTIONS

Lowercase	user-supplied information
Uppercase	explicit portions of dBase II commands
[...]	optional portions of dBase II commands
<...>	user-supplied portions of dBase II commands

FILE NAMING CONVENTIONS

File names may be up to 8 characters (no spaces) long.

FIELD NAMING CONVENTIONS

Field names may be up to 10 characters (no spaces) long, must start with a letter, but can include digits and embedded colons.

dBase II DATA TYPES

C Character data. Includes any printable console (ASCII) character.
N Numeric data for calculation. Includes numbers, +, -,.
L Logical data. Includes Y,y,T,t for True, or N,n,F,f for False.

CURSOR MOVEMENT AND CONTROL KEYS
FULL-SCREEN OPERATION (all modes):

For special controls used in conjunction with Edit, Modify, Append, Create or Insert.

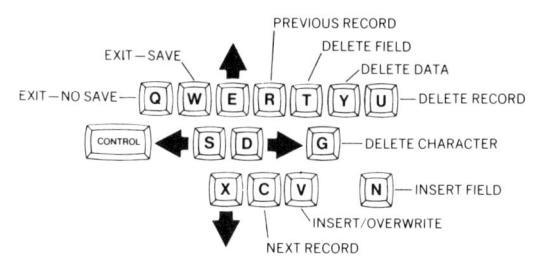

dBase II FILE TYPES

.CMD	command file
.DBF	database file
.FMT	format file
.FRM	report form file
.MEM	memory file
.NDX	index file
.TXT	text output

TERMINOLOGY

<commands> or <statements> any valid dBase command or function.

<cstring> character string(s). In most instances must be delimited with single quotes (''), double quotes (""), or brackets ([ ]).

<cstring exp> an <exp> whose content is defined as Character in type. May be a cstring, a memvar or field with character content, or any combination of these items and operators.

<delimiter> any non-alphanumeric character used to demarcate data, e.g., single quotes (''), double quotes (""), brackets ([ ]), colons (::), commas (,,), etc.

<exp> or <expression> an item or group of items and operators whose value can be determined by dBASE II. <exp>s may be defined as C, N, or L depending upon the "type" of data they contain.

<exp list> a list of expressions delimited with commas.

<field> a record field name.

<field list> a list of field names delimited with commas.

<file> name of file you wish to create or access.

<index file> name of index file you wish to create or access.

<key> the portion(s) of a database file used to create an index file.

Summary of dBase II Commands

<**memvar**>   the name of a memory variable.

<**memvar list**>   list of memory variables delimited with commas.

<**n**>   a number which dBase II regards as a literal value.

<**numeric exp**>   an <exp> whose content is defined as Numeric.

<**scope**>   command option specifies range of records dBase II must treat in executing command. <scope> has three possible values: ALL records in file; NEXT n records in file; and RECORD n. Default value varies from command to command.

<**skeleton**>   allows batch manipulation of files of same type and/or with matching cstring in filename; allows batch manipulation of groups of <memvars> with matching cstring in name.

OPERATORS used for data manipulation.

Logical Operators (listed in order of precedence)

()	parentheses for grouping
.NOT.	logical not (unary operator)
.AND.	logical and
.OR.	logical or
$	substring logical operator

Arithmetic Operators (listed in order of precedence)

()	parentheses for grouping
*	multiplication
/	division
+	addition
—	subtraction

Relational Operators

&lt;	less than
&gt;	greater than
=	equal to
<>	not equal to
<=	less than or equal to
>=	greater than or equal to

String Operators

+   string concatenation
−   string concatenation with blank squash

FUNCTIONS

★

deleted record function evaluates as a logical True if current record is marked for deletion.

#

record pointer (a system memory variable) stores the number of the current record.

&

macro function permits the use of a <memvar>'s stored value in a command line. (<memvar>'s value must be a 'cstring'.)

! (<cstring exp>)

upper case function converts all lower case characters to upper case.

$ (<exp>, <start>, <length>)

substring function extracts the specified part of <exp> from the given starting position for the given length.

@ (<cstring exp 1>, <cstring exp 2>)

substring search function yields an integer value indicating where the first string appears in the second.

CHR (<numeric exp>)

yields the ASCII character equivalent of a numeric expression.

DATE ( )

name of system variable containing the system date.

EOF

End-Of-File function evaluates as a logical True when last record of USE file has been surpassed.

FILE (<file>)

file function evaluates as a logical True if named file exists on disk in use.

INT (<numeric exp>)

integer function truncates everything to the right of the decimal to form an integer.

LEN (<cstring exp>)

length function returns the number of characters in the specified <cstring exp>.

RANK (<cstring exp>)
returns the (ASCII numeric) value of the leftmost character of <cstring exp>.

STR (<numeric exp>, <length>, [<decimals>])
string function converts specified portion of <numeric exp> into a cstring.

TRIM (<cstring exp>)
trim function removes trailing blanks from specified cstring.

TYPE (<exp>)
type function indicates data "type" of indicated <exp>.

VAL (<cstring exp>)
value function converts a cstring (composed of numerals) into a numeric expression.

dBase II COMMANDS

? <exp>
evaluates and displays value of <exp>.

@ <coord> [SAY <exp> [USING 'picture']] [GET <var> [PICTURE 'picture']]
format console screen or printer output.

ACCEPT ['prompt'] TO <memvar>
prompts user to input cstring into specified <memvar>. Input requires no quotes.

APPEND [BLANK]
add record(s) or blank, formatted record to database file.

APPEND FROM <file> [SDF] or [DELIMITED] [FOR <exp>] [WHILE <exp>]
appends data from a database or system data format file into database file in use.

BROWSE [FIELDS <field list>]
allows full screen "window" viewing and editing of database file in use.

Call <memvar>
machine language command.

CANCEL
aborts command file execution.

CHANGE [<scope>] FIELD <list> [FOR <exp>]
permits selective editing of records by field.

Working With dBase II

CLEAR [GETS]
"resets" dBase.

CONTINUE
continues a LOCATE command.

COPY TO <file> STRUCTURE [EXTENDED] [FIELD <list>]
copies structure of file in use to designated file.

COPY TO <file> [<scope>] [FIELD <list>] [FOR <exp>] [WHILE <exp>]
copies file in use to designated database file.

COPY TO <file> [<scope>] [FIELD <list>] [SDF] [DELIMITED [WITH <delimiter>]] [FOR <exp>] [WHILE <exp>]]
copies data from file in use to file with designated name and format.

COPY TO <file> STRUCTURE EXTENDED
creates a database file whose records represent the structure of the file in use.

COUNT [<scope>] [FOR <exp>] [WHILE <exp>] [TO <memvar>]
counts records that satisfy some condition. Default value is all records.

CREATE [<file>]
initiates creation of database file.

CREATE <newfile> FROM <oldfile>
creates database file whose structure is determined by the data contained in the records of the <oldfile>. (Used with COPY STRUCTURE EXTENDED.)

DELETE [<scope>] [FOR <exp>] [WHILE <exp>]
marks specified records for deletion.

DELETE FILE <file>
deletes specified file.

DISPLAY [<scope>] [<field list>] [FOR <exp>] [WHILE <exp>] [OFF]
displays records of database file in use.

DISPLAY FILES [ON <disk drive>] [LIKE <skeleton>]
displays files on disk. Default values: database files, logged drive.

DISPLAY MEMORY
displays current <memvars>s.

DISPLAY STATUS
displays system information: e.g., system date, files open, index files and keys, and all SET parameters.

DISPLAY STRUCTURE
displays structure of file in use.

EDIT [n]
initiates selective editing of database file in use.

EJECT
commands printer to perform a form feed (eject page).

ERASE
clears console screen.

FIND <cstring>
locates first record in indexed database file whose <key> matches the specified <cstring>.

GO or GOTO <n> or <TOP>, or <BOTTOM>
positions to specific record or place in the database file in use.

HELP [<command verb or other entry>]
accesses Help File overview or specific Help File entry for brief explanation of specified command mode, function, etc.

INDEX ON <key> TO <file>
creates an index file for the database in use.

INPUT ['prompt'] TO <memvar>
prompts user to enter <exp> into already named <memvar>.

INSERT [BEFORE] [BLANK]
inserts a new record anywhere in database file.

JOIN TO <file> FOR <exp> [FIELDS <list>]
creates new database file by merging records of files in use in Primary and Secondary areas for which FOR <exp> evaluates as a logical True.

LIST [<scope>] [<field list>] [FOR <exp>] [WHILE <exp>] [OFF]
lists records of file in use.

LIST FILES [ON <disk drive>] [LIKE <skeleton>]
lists files on disk. Default values: logged drive, database files.

LIST MEMORY
lists current <memvars>.

LIST STATUS
lists system information: e.g., system date, files open, index files and keys, and all SET parameters.

LIST STRUCTURE
displays structure of file in use.

LOCATE [<scope>] [FOR <exp>]
finds first record which satisfies specified condition. Use **CONTINUE** to reach next such record.

LOOP
MODIFY COMMAND <file>
calls dBase II's text editor and brings up designated file for modification.

MODIFY STRUCTURE
allows structural modification of database file in use.

NOTE or *
commands dBase II not to read the rest of command line. Used to insert programming comments in command files.

PACK
eliminates records marked for deletion.

QUIT [TO <list CP/M level commands or .COM files>]
terminates dBase II and returns control to operating system. Optionally calls system level programs.

READ
initiates full-screen editing of a formatted screen, and accepts data into GET commands.

RECALL [<scope>] [FOR <exp>] [WHILE <exp>]
reinstates records previously marked for deletion.

REINDEX
updates index files not in use during alteration of corresponding database file.

RELEASE [<memvar list>] or [ALL] or [ALL LIKE <skeleton>] or [ALL EXCEPT <skeleton>]
eliminates unwanted <memvars> from current memory.

REMARK
permits display of following characters. In command file is used to output comments to screen or print.

RENAME <oldfile> TO <newfile>
permits renaming of file.

REPLACE [<scope>] <field> WITH <exp> [,<field2> WITH <exp2>...] [FOR <exp>] [WHILE <exp>]
replaces the value of specified fields of specified records with stated values.

REPORT [FORM <filename>] [<scope>] [FOR <exp>] [WHILE <exp>] [TO PRINT] [PLAIN]

generates or accesses existing Report Form File for output of data in user-defined format.

RESET [<drive>]
resets CP/M after disk swap.

RESTORE FROM <file> [ADDITIVE]
retrieves and activates <memvars> previously saved in .MEM file. Deletes all current <memvars> unless Additive option employed.

RETURN
terminates a command file and returns control to calling file or interactive mode.

SAVE TO <file> [ALL LIKE <skeleton>] [ALL EXCEPT <skeleton>]
saves all current (designated) <memvars> to .MEM file.

SELECT [PRIMARY] or [SECONDARY]
switches between dBase II's primary and secondary work areas.

SET
see below for all SET commands.

SKIP [+/— n]
moves forward or backwards through the records of the file in use. Default value: +1, +n.

SORT ON <key> TO <file> [ASCENDING] or [DESCENDING]
creates a version of the database file in use whose records are arranged alphabetically or numerically according to the information contained in the field specified as the SORT <key>. Default value: ascending.

STORE <exp> TO <memvar>
computes the value of <exp> and stores it to the designated <memvar>.

SUM <field list> [TO <memvar list>] [<scope>] [FOR <exp>] [WHILE <exp>]
computes and displays the sum of numeric fields.

TEXT/ENDTEXT

TOTAL TO <file> ON <key> [FIELDS <field list>] [FOR <exp>] [WHILE <exp>]
generates a summary version of an indexed or pre-sorted database file which contains the totals of numeric fields for records (in the use file) bearing the same <key>.

UPDATE FROM <filename> ON <key> [ADD <field list>] or [REPLACE <field list>] or [REPLACE <field> WITH <field>] [RANDOM]
allows batch update of file in use by drawing upon information from designated FROM file.

USE <file> [INDEX <file list>]
opens a database file and (optionally) engages desired index files.

WAIT [TO <memvar>]
suspends dBase II operation until a single console character is entered; optionally stores the latter to a designated <memvar>.

SET COMMANDS

The default value of each SET command of ON/OFF type is indicated by order of presentation: OFF/ON indicates default value of OFF; ON/OFF a default value of ON.

SET ALTERNATE TO [<file>]
creates designated file (type .TXT) for saving screen output to disk. Repeated without [<file>], closes .TXT file.

SET ALTERNATE OFF/ON
ON sends screen output to disk file created with previous command; OFF shuts off output.

SET BELL ON/OFF
ON rings bell when invalid data entered or field boundary passed; OFF turns off bell.

SET CARRY OFF/ON
When using APPEND (full-screen), ON enters data from last record into present record; OFF turns off function.

SET COLON ON/OFF
ON displays colons which delimit or bound input variables; OFF hides colons.

SET CONFIRM OFF/ON
ON waits for <return> before skipping to next field in full-screen mode; OFF skips to next field as soon as present field is filled.

SET CONSOLE ON/OFF
ON sends all output to screen; OFF suspends all output to screen.

SET DATE TO <MM/DD/YY>
sets or resets system date.

SET DEBUG OFF/ON
ON sends output from SET ECHO and STEP to print; OFF sends output to screen.

SET DEFAULT TO <drive>
commands dBase II to regard specified drive as default drive for all future operations.

SET DELETED OFF/ON
ON prevents dBase II from reading/processing any record marked for deletion following a command which has <scope> as an option. OFF allows dBase II to read all records.

SET ECHO OFF/ON
ON allows monitoring of command file execution by echoing all commands to screen; OFF suppresses echo.

SET EJECT ON/OFF
ON causes REPORT command to trigger a form-feed (page eject) before sending report to print; OFF disables the page eject.

SET ESCAPE ON/OFF
ON enables user to abort command file execution by hitting ESCape key; OFF disables ESC key.

SET EXACT OFF/ON
ON requires exact match in any comparison between two strings (e.g., in use of FOR <exp> or FIND command); OFF allows matches between strings of different lengths.

SET FORMAT TO [<file>]
accesses specified file (type .FMT) containing custom made screen/print format for use in conjunction with APPEND, EDIT, INSERT, etc.

SET FORMAT TO <screen/print>
directs output from format file to screen or printer.

SET HEADING TO <cstring>
saves <cstring> internally and inserts it as REPORT header line. (cstring limited to 60 chars.)

SET INDEX TO [<file list>]
sets up index files for use with corresponding database file. First listed .NDX file will be engaged as the active index; all other .NDX files will be automatically updated to reflect any changes to the database file.

SET INTENSITY ON/OFF
ON enables inverse video or dual intensity during full-screen operations (if hardware permits); OFF disables these features.

SET LINKAGE OFF/ON
ON enables simultaneous movement of record pointers in both Primary and Secondary work areas in response to commands which only permit downward movement through a file (i.e., command with <scope>). OFF suspends pointer linkage.

SET MARGIN TO <n>
sets left hand margin of printer to <n>.

166 *Working With dBase II*

SET PRINT OFF/ON
ON directs output to printer; OFF cuts off output to printer.

SET RAW OFF/ON
ON LISTs and DISPLAYs records without inserting spaces between fields; OFF inserts an extra space between fields.

SET SCREEN ON/OFF
ON enables full-screen operation with APPEND, EDIT, CREATE, etc. OFF disables full-screen operation.

SET STEP OFF/ON
ON aids debugging of command files by halting execution after performing each command; OFF disables STEP.

SET TALK ON/OFF
ON displays results of commands on screen; OFF suppresses display of results.

STRUCTURED PROGRAMMING COMMANDS

DO <file>
accesses and executes a command file (type .CMD).

DO CASE permits choice of one and only one of several
   CASE <exp1> possible execution paths, i.e., CASE <expl>
      <statements> through CASE <expN>. When CASE <exp>
   CASE <exp2> evaluates as logically True, the following
      <statements> statements and commands will be performed.
   CASE <expN>
      <statements>
   OTHERWISE OTHERWISE clause for alternate execution
      <statements> path is optional. DO CASE structure must be
   OTHERWISE terminated with ENDCASE.
      <statements>
ENDCASE

DO WHILE <exp>
      <statements>
   LOOP opens a structured command loop. The
      <statements> following commands and statements will be
ENDDO executed until <exp> evaluates as a logical False. An optional portion of DO WHILE, LOOP causes command file to jump back and re-evaluate DO WHILE <exp>. Structure must terminate with ENDO.

   IF <exp> permits conditional execution of following
      <statements> statements and commands. Optional ELSE

Summary of dBase II Commands 167

ELSE   provides an alternate path of execution.
    <statements> Structure must terminate with ENDIF
ENDIF

TEXT   allows the output of text information from a
    <any text>   command file. dBase II will read everything as
ENDTEXT   text for output until it encounters an END-
                                      TEXT command.

Appendix D
dBase II Constraints

Maximum fields per record	32
Maximum characters per record	1000
Maximum records per database	65535
Maximum characters per character string	254
Maximum characters in an index key	99
Maximum characters in a REPORT header	254
Maximum characters per command line	254
Maximum expressions in a SUM command	5
Maximum pending GETS	64
Maximum memory variables	64
Maximum files open at a time	16
Largest number	approx. 1.8×10^{63}
Smallest number	approx. 1.0×10^{-63}
Accuracy of numeric fields	10 digits

Index

! function, 33, 133
# function, 85, 129
$ function, 20, 30, 56, 123,-7, 130, 138-9, 143
$ operator, 34, 141-2
& , 77, 90, 110-14, 119
* , 70, 97, 144
* function, 129
+ operator, 30, 76, 78, 82
.CMD file, 68, 97
.DBF file, 13, 27, 32
.FMT file, 96-7, 139
.FRM file, 22-3, 26, 27
.MEM file, 115-16, 120
.NDX file, 28-9
.NOT. operator, 21, 124
.PRG file, 68, 97
.TXT file, 135, 146-7, 148
1-2-3, 147
?, 38-9, 71, 74, 105, 109, 111
??, 71
@, 71-80, 82-3, 87-90, 92, 96-9, 102-103, 105, 117, 138, 140-41
@ function, 133, 143

abstat, 151
ACCEPT, 102
ADDITIVE keyword, 116, 120
adhesive labels, 104
ALL keyword, 37, 47, 48, 115
APPEND, 13-16, 31, 43, 50-51, 92, 118-19, 139
APPEND BLANK, 92
APPEND FROM, 59, 61, 147
ascending sequence, 29, 32
Ashton-Tate, 6
autocode, 149

BOTTOM keyword, 34
BROWSE, 31, 48-9, 51

CANCEL, 103
CASE, 101-102
CHANGE, 31, 48, 51
character field, 11, 20, 72, 87, 102
CHR function, 134
CLEAR, 59, 102-103, 114
CLEAR GETS, 102, 140-41
close file, 15
colon, 13
column heading, 25
command file, 6, 67-70, 75, 80, 83, 87, 100, 116, 124
comparison operators, 21
CONTINUE, 34, 36
COPY, 33, 45-6, 51, 59, 118-19, 146-7
COPY STRUCTURE, 54
COUNT, 37-9, 46, 51
counting, 37-9
CP/M, 5, 7, 11, 46, 68, 115
CP/M-80, 6
CP/M-86, 6
CREATE, 11-12, 14, 19, 20, 25, 54
current record, 22, 33, 35, 45, 78
current record number, 14, 85, 129
cursor control, 15, 16, 17, 49, 50-51, 95

data entry, 12-16
data sequence, 28-33
database file, 9-12, 13
date, 55, 88, 118, 123-7, 133-4
DATE () function, 123-5, 133
dBase II editor, 26, 67, 97
dBase II RunTime, 151
DBASEMSG.TXT, 10
DBPlus, 150
decimals, 13-14
DELETE, 44-6
DELETE FILE, 46, 51
deleted record, 17, 44-7
deleted record function, 129

170 Index

deletion marker, 18, 38, 45-6
DELIMITED keyword, 146-7
DESCENDING keyword, 32
descending sequence, 29, 32
dGraph, 150
DISPLAY, 21-2, 33, 34, 36, 58, 68, 69-70
DISPLAY FILES, 27
DISPLAY MEMORY, 38, 117
DISPLAY STATUS, 31
DISPLAY STRUCTURE, 8, 13, 37, 51
DO, 83
DO CASE, 100-101
DO loop, 87, 119, 125-6
DO WHILE, 69, 79, 83, 84, 124-5
DO WHILE T, 86
documentation, 143-5
DOS, 6, 7, 11, 46, 68, 115, 133
duplicate records, 140
dUtil, 150

EDIT, 16, 18, 31, 33, 48-9, 51, 53, 139
editing, 16-18, 47-9
editing rules, 15, 68, 95
EJECT, 73-4, 76, 109
ELSE, 85, 87, 94
end of file, 69, 79
ENDCASE, 101
ENDDO, 69, 79, 83, 126
ENDIF, 69, 87
ENDTEXT, 109
enquiry program, 81
EOF function, 129
ERASE, 86, 94, 127
error correction, 8
error messages, 7

field, 10, 19, 28, 40
FIELD keyword, 59-60
field size, 11-12, 72, 87-8
field type, 11-12, 74
fieldname, 11, 13, 111, 112, 144-5
file, 9-12, 28, 32, 33
file create, 11-12
File function, 119, 129
file location, 27
file size, 10
file structure, 37, 51
filename, 11, 12, 67, 115, 119
FIND, 35-6, 55, 57, 58, 77, 82, 85, 87, 110, 140
FOR keyword, 20, 36-7, 39, 47, 48, 60-61, 69
FORM keyword, 22-3

format file, 96-9
formatting characters, 88-90
FROM keyword, 55
functions, 128-34

GET keyword, 87-8, 95, 140-41
GO, 34, 139
GO BOTTOM, 34
GO TOP, 34
GOTO, 22, 34, 43

head of form, 73
HELP, 8
HELP file, 10

IBM PC, 6, 10
IF, 69-70, 74, 87
indentation, 76, 144
index, 25, 35, 43, 58
INDEX, 28-33, 43, 118
index file, 28-9
indexing, 28-33
initialing variables, 138-9
INPUT, 102, 111, 117
INSERT, 33, 43, 92
INSERT BEFORE, 43
INSERT BLANK, 44
insert mode, 15, 17, 18
INT function, 126-7, 130
Intel 8080 processor, 6
Intel 8086 processor, 6
Intel 8088 processor, 6
invoicing, 117-22

JOIN, 61-2

labels, 103-108
LEN function, 132
letter, 108
LIKE keyword, 27, 115
line positioning, 76
lines per page, 24
LIST, 19-22, 36, 51, 68
LIST FILES, 27
listing data, 19-27
LOCATE, 34-5, 36, 68
logical expressions, 84
logical field, 12, 87, 102, 104, 124
logical memory variable, 72
logical operators, 21
long commands, 93
LOOP, 87
lower-case, 13, 32-3, 88

Index

macro substitute character, 77, 90, 119
macro substitution, 110–14, 142
Mailmerge, 148
margin, 24
memory variable, 37–8, 71–2, 76–8, 84, 87, 92, 102, 104, 111, 112, 114–17
menu, 81, 99–102
MODIFY COMMAND, 26, 59, 67–8
MODIFY STRUCTURE, 50–51
MS–DOS, 6

names and addresses, 103–108
negative values, 12, 14, 38
nesting, 100
NEXT keyword, 21, 23, 34, 35–6, 37, 48, 60
NOTE, 70, 144
numeric field, 11–12, 20, 30, 38, 40, 72, 87, 102

OFF keyword, 21
ON keyword, 27, 55
OTHERWISE, 101–102

PACK, 31, 33, 46–7
page heading, 24
page width, 24
passwords, 141
PC–DOS, 6, 68
PICTURE keyword, 88–9, 103, 124
PLAIN keyword, 23
primary database, 57–62
Printer, 19, 23, 74
Programming, 67–127
Prompt, 7

quickcode, 149
QUIT, 12, 16, 26, 98, 114

RANDOM keyword, 55
RANK function, 134
READ, 82, 92, 95, 96–8, 102, 124, 140–41
RECALL, 45
record, 10
record number, 16, 17, 21, 33–6, 85
RELEASE, 114–15
REMARK, 144
RENAME, 46, 50–51
REPLACE, 31, 47–8, 51, 92, 95
REPLACE keyword, 55–6
REPORT, 22–6, 36, 68
report file, 22–3
RESTORE, 115–16, 120
RETURN, 80, 85, 86, 103, 114

RunTime, 151

SAVE, 115–17, 120
SAY keyword, 71–80, 82–3, 87–90
screen clearing, 86
screen formatting, 139
screen validation, 140–41
SDF keyword, 146–7
secondary database, 57–62
SELECT PRIMARY, 58–9, 77, 120
SELECT SECONDARY, 58, 77, 120
selection criteria, 21, 23, 34, 48
semicolon, 93
SET ALTERNATE, 148
SET CARRY, 16, 54–5
SET commands, 135–8
SET CONSOLE, 141
SET DATE TO, 26, 125, 133
SET DEFAULT TO, 27
SET DELETED, 35, 37
SET FORMAT TO, 74, 96–9, 139
SET HEADING TO, 26
SET INDEX TO, 31
SET PRINT, 19, 74
SET TALK, 70, 74
Sirius, 6
SKIP, 33–4, 35, 36, 69, 70, 74, 76
software files, 10
software releases, 6
SORT, 32–3
sorting, 25, 28, 32–3
spreadsheet, 146–8
STORE, 73, 82, 112, 120, 124, 133, 138
STR function, 30, 72, 76, 130, 138
sub-totalling, 24, 39–40
Substring function, 20, 30, 32, 56, 123–7, 130, 138–9, 143
Substring operator, 34, 141–2
SUM, 38–9, 46, 51, 68
Superbrain, 6
Supercalc, 147–8

temporary field, 37–8, 71
TEXT, 109
TO PRINT keyword, 23
TOP keyword, 34
TOTAL, 39–40, 140
totalling, 24, 26, 38–40
TRIM function, 20, 87, 105, 132, 142–3
TRS–80II, 6
TYPE function, 134

underlining, 24, 25
UPDATE, 55–7

upper-case, 13, 32-3, 88
USE, 13, 15, 16, 28, 30-31, 33, 34, 51-2, 57, 59, 119
USING keyword, 88-90

VAL function, 123-7, 131
validation, 141-2
Victor 9000, 6

WAIT, 86
WAIT TO, 140
WHILE keyword, 36-7, 60-61
WITH keyword, 146-7
word processor, 26, 97, 109, 145, 146-8
Wordstar, 148

Zilog Z80 processor, 6
zip, 149